...terey, California 1842.

17. Juan Malarin
18. Charles Wolter
19. Nathan Spear
20. John B. R. Cooper
21. G. de la Torre –
22. Jose R. Estrada
23. Rafael Gonzales
24. Wreck Com. Rodgers
... Yorktown, Schr California.

25. Government Buildings
26. Mariano Estrada
27. Joaquin Gomez
28. Ruins old Presidio
29. Road Pueblo de San Jose
30. Mexican Fort –
31. Simeon Castro
32. Antonio Osio
33. James Stokes

COOPER

Juan Bautista Rogers Cooper

Sea Captain □ *Adventurer* □ *Ranchero*
and
Early California Pioneer

1791—1872

John Woolfenden
and
Amelie Elkinton

THE BOXWOOD PRESS

Distributed by

THE BOXWOOD PRESS
183 Ocean View Blvd.
Pacific Grove, CA 93950

408—375-9110

Library of Congress Cataloging in Publication Data

Woolfenden, John.
  Cooper: Juan Bautista Rogers Cooper, sea captain, adventurer, ranchero,
and early California pioneer, 1791-1872.

  Bibliography: p.
  Includes index.
  1. Cooper, Juan Bautista Rogers, 1791-1872. 2. Pioneers—California—
Biography. 3. California—Biography. 4. California—History.
  I. Elkinton, Amelie. II. Title.

F864.C74W66 1983   979.4'04   83—22430

ISBN: 0-910286-95-7

Printed in U.S.A.

PREFACE

ONE DAY some years ago I stood in a room of the ancestral home of Miss Frances Molera in downtown Monterey, now known as the Cooper-Molera Adobe, and realized that the biography of her celebrated grandfather, Capt. John B.R. Cooper, had yet to be written. Before me were old account books of the family, some dating from the 1820s, and around the room were assorted mounds of books and old periodicals of the 1800s which the family had saved.

Miss Molera died in October 1968, willing her family home to the National Trust for Historic Preservation. Several committees were appointed by the president of the Monterey History and Art Association to work with the executor and the National Trust representatives in compiling a preliminary listing of the house contents before temporary storage.

A lease was signed between the National Trust and the State of California Department of Parks and Recreation, whereby the State would develop the property and the National Trust would act in an advisory capacity.

A chronological file was started regarding Capt. Cooper and his family, which I hoped would be the basis for his biography. About the same time, Hazel Dittmer, a local author, also became interested in his life. She wrote several articles for the History and Art Association publication, *Noticias del Puerto de Monterey,* and we visited together several source libraries. Unfortunately, Hazel's sudden death precluded a firm commitment to publication.

Since then the file has continued to grow, spilling over into several large storage-file boxes. The search has ranged from Massachusetts to Honolulu and various parts of California.

A year ago John Woolfenden, a retired newspaperman and writer of many magazine articles and two books on the Monterey

Peninsula area, was induced to read the material and became keenly interested. Now the hundreds of pieces of the jigsaw puzzle which constitutes the story of Juan Bautista Rogers Cooper may emerge from the shadowy background of California history to help him take his place with his contemporaries. Here was a sea captain who sailed thousands of miles over the Pacific Ocean. He married into an early California family. He developed thousands of acres of rancho lands. He brought to California his younger half-brother, Thomas O. Larkin, whose papers are the basis for much of California's recorded history. Capt. Cooper participated vitally in the development of the Golden State, accepting the best of the old customs and contributing in great part to the new.

Amelie Elkinton

Carmel Valley, California
1983

TWO LARGE FILE BOXES labeled "Chronology" and "Excerpts" introduced me to research material, gathered painstakingly over a period of a dozen years or more by Amelie Elkinton and the late Hazel Dittmer, on the life of Juan Bautista Rogers Cooper.

Before I was acquainted with this mass of data, I had included a brief biography of Capt. Cooper in one of the chapters of a previous book, *Big Sur: A Battle for the Wilderness,* published by Boxwood Press in 1981. And I had asked Mrs. Elkinton if she would be willing to check the manuscript of that book for historical accuracy.

Protesting that she was not an expert on Big Sur, she nevertheless read the script and made a few corrections, then asked me if I would be interested in writing the complete story of Cooper, who, she believed, had been neglected by most historians in favor of his half-brother, Thomas Oliver Larkin. She then showed me the two file boxes, which I took home and started to read.

What I discovered later was that she had all sorts of additional boxes, files, folders, envelopes, and cartons of all descriptions, containing letters, maps, memoranda, account books, and documents of all kinds that overflowed the closets of her apartment in Carmel Valley Manor.

We began meeting on Thursday mornings, as I started trying to make a narrative out of all this miscellany, and she set to work to answer my hundreds of queries regarding the missing links.

I never went home from one of those meetings without carrying at least one reference book from the Elkinton shelves. If she thought I was becoming overburdened with books, she would say, "I think your wife would be interested in this."

My wife and I wallowed in rare Californiana. It was amazing how many of the early Californians had known Cooper, and had comments about him, most of them highly complimentary. Which you will see if you spend an hour or two with this, the most complete biography of him, to date.

Most of chapter one appeared originally as a feature article in the Weekend Magazine section of the Monterey Peninsula Herald, whose management gave permission for it to be repeated here. I wish to thank also Robert Reese, historian of the State Parks Department, for his cooperation in making it possible to photograph Cooper memorabilia, and for reading and checking the manuscript.

John Woolfenden

Carmel Valley, California
1983

CONTENTS

Captain Juan Bautista Rogers Cooper, born September, 1791, and baptized as John Rogers Cooper at St. Anne's Parish Church, Alderney, English Channel Islands. Also baptized in Roman Catholic Church at Royal Presidio chapel, Monterey, California, April 14, 1827, with William E.P. Hartnell as sponsor. Died February 9, 1872, San Francisco, leaving two sons and two daughters as well as his widow Encarnacion. (Elkinton collection.)

1

THE FATE OF THE "CRANKY SCHOONER"

O F ALL THE SHIPS which sailed the Pacific during the days of Mexican rule in California, the schooner *California* was undoubtedly the most unpredictable. Whether she would make it to her next port of call was always a question.

She first arrived in Monterey, June 10, 1837, having been brought from Honolulu by Captain Henry Paty, who named this 83-ton vessel the *Clarion*. At some point in her Hawaiian life she had also been known as the *Kaniu*. When Paty sold her to California Governor Juan Bautista Alvarado, she was rechristened the *California,* as befitted a Mexican ship which was to be used to take government officials, mail, prisoners, etc., between Monterey and San Blas, the port on Mexico's west coast which connected most directly with Mexico City.

The sale price was $9,000, of which $6,424 was the duty charged on her cargo. The balance was to be paid in hides and tallow in two months, during which Paty was to remain in command.

Since the government in Mexico City rarely had any money to be wasted on that far-away province of Alta California, which was expected to be self-sufficient, cash was a rare commodity in the capital city of Monterey. Whether Paty ever received his hides and tallow is not recorded, but when the two months were up, Thomas M. Robbins was named captain and the *California* sailed August 25 for San Blas on government business. It was more than a year before she returned, November 13, 1838, and presumably she had to be patched up considerably before she could leave San Blas, as "expenses" by April 30, 1839, were listed as $8,000 above and beyond the purchase price.

1

In January, 1839, she had been used as a prison ship, and though there are no details of that particular voyage, Sir George Simpson, governor in chief of the Hudson's Bay Company's territories in North America, wrote in his *Voyages to California Ports, 1841-42,* that on another occasion the schooner had on board seven convicts, "if men who had not been tried could be so called, who were to be transported by order of the executive government on charges of murder and robbery, and to be left, as was supposed, on the uninhabited island of Santa Guadalupe, lying to the south of San Diego."

A new captain came aboard the *California* on April 18, 1839. He was Juan Bautista Rogers Cooper, who knew all about Mexican methods of payment. In 1823 as master of the *Rover,* Cooper sailed from Boston for California via the Sandwich (Hawaiian) Islands. He eventually sold the *Rover* to Governor Luis Antonio Arguello of California, remaining as captain on voyages to Hawaii and to Canton, China, with the right to trade on his own account. He and Arguello got into an argument as to Cooper's share of the sales, Cooper won his case in an arbitration court, but had to relinquish the ship.

So at age 35, having spent more than half of his life up to that time, at sea, Cooper decided to settle down on shore and open a general merchandise store in Monterey. He also began putting together a considerable and widespread "empire" of land grants, extending from Big Sur to Sonoma County.

His expenses, however, frequently exceeded his income, and the difficulties of hiring competent help, of coping with alternate years of drought and flood, of wheeling and dealing in hides and tallow, in otter skins and household goods, left him perennially short of cash.

Therefore Cooper made a deal with Governor Alvarado. He would command the *California,* but once again he was to have the right to trade on his own.

His first short trip, to San Diego, had Andres Castillero as a passenger. Castillero had brought the news earlier from Mexico

City that Alvarado had been confirmed as governor, by a government which had previously named Carlos Carrillo to that office, then changed its mind when Alvarado refused to recognize Carrillo.

In May the *California* returned to Monterey and stayed on the coast, though an effort was made to send her to the Islands, apparently unsuccessfully. As Sir George Simpson observed, this was a cranky schooner, constantly in need of repairs. In June she made a trip to Acapulco, was damaged in a storm, and at the end of October put into San Francisco Bay during a gale, not being totally seaworthy.

In January, 1840, Cooper had orders to go to San Diego to pick up a cargo of hides for Honolulu. He was told that he could devote the proceeds to repairs, or could exchange the vessel for another, paying up to $5,000. So on March 16 the schooner sailed from San Diego. No deal was made for an exchange, and during April, May and June, repairs costing $2,222 were made in Honolulu, then the Gibraltar of the Pacific, with the only dependable shipyards. While the repairs were being made, Cooper signed an agreement with the governor of Oahu, Kekuanara, to take on six Kanaka crewmen. He and the native Hawaiians had always got along well aboard ship. The cargo he brought back included doors, windows, honey, and a four-wheeled carriage.

In December of that year, Cooper's half-brother, Thomas Oliver Larkin, leased the ship for a voyage to Acapulco, going along himself to keep an eye on his cargo. It was June, 1841, when the *California* got back to Monterey. From September to December it lay at Sausalito while Cooper visited two of his ranches, at Nicasio and Punta de Quentin.

In 1842 the log shows John Roderick as mate, with a crew of 14, "all foreigners but two." The foreigners were Kanakas, Chilenos, and two New Zealand Maoris.

"This national vessel, a mere apology for a coasting cruiser," wrote Simpson, "is an old cranky craft, not mounting a single gun, and so badly manned that she is unable to make any progress by beating against the wind. I have mentioned that the skipper's wife, a sister of General Vallejo, resides at Sonoma, so that as soon as he anchors in Whaler's Harbor (Sausalito) Captain Cooper starts off with the boat and the bulk of the crew across San Pablo Bay to see his friends, and as the victualing depart-ment, which is never in a flourishing condition, is peculiarly low at the end of a voyage, the mate has been known to starve three days in sight of herds of cattle."

At another point in his narrative, Sir George writes of arriving at Lahaina, Maui, where "we found ourselves in company with nine American whalers and our old friend Captain Cooper who had just arrived from Acapulco in his cranky schooner."

It was a wonder that the *California* could continue to make the run from Acapulco to Monterey and back. In 1842 the log shows expenses of $2,831, "Besides $6,428 paid to Peirce and Brewer for previous repairs."

It was in October, 1842, that this lone Mexican "naval" vessel on the California Coast was nearly put out of commission by the United States Navy.

The *California* had just returned from a voyage to Acapulco, San Blas, and Mazatlan. Foreigners had been moving into Cali-fornia in increasing numbers and in Monterey it was considered only a matter of time before either Great Britain or the United States moved into the situation. There was no contingency plan, however, for such an event.

Under the mistaken belief that Mexico and the U.S. were at war, Commodore Thomas ap Catesby Jones sailed his ship, the *United States*, into Monterey Bay, believing that he had also beaten the British at seizing the territory, as a British fleet under Rear Admiral Richard Thomas was thought to be racing Jones from Callao, Peru.

Jones had the Mexican flag hauled down at the Monterey Custom House and replaced by the Stars and Stripes. At the same time, he boarded and seized the *California*.

In a book published in 1871, *Forward and Aft,* W.D. Phelps

described Cooper's reaction to the seizure of his ship:

> On hearing the news he rushed out of doors, and beholding the changes scratched his left elbow with his right hand, which operation was always indicative of unusual and immense excitement. His neighbors, anticipating some extraordinary outburst of passion, awaited the explosion....His only sorrow was expressed in another scratch at his elbow, and "Well, I wouldn't care a snap for the loss of the old schooner, if I had only got a well-rope out of her first." He had been digging a well, and a rope for the bucket was needed...

Jones sent Captain James Armstrong ashore to demand from Governor Alvarado the surrender of Monterey and California by 9 o'clock the next morning.

Advised by Captain Mariano Silva, commandant of the Monterey Castillo, that the town's defenses were in no shape to resist, Alvarado sent Captain Pedro Narvaez and Jose Abrego, representing the military and civil governments, to Jones' flagship, with Thomas O. Larkin as interpreter, and retired to his ranch at Alisal. The next morning, the Americans landed and marched through town with bands playing, but Larkin, though he was not named U.S. consul until the following year, had important connections in New York and Washington, and was able to show Jones recent correpondence which made no mention of war. Jones was finally persuaded that he had been a bit hasty in annexing California and agreed to withdraw. There were various parties in town that night for the Americans, who marched out the following day with bands playing once more and the Mexican flag restored to its righful place.

The *California* was returned to Cooper, who presumably retrieved his well-rope as his first action aboard.

He had had trouble enough on his previous voyage. An epidemic of smallpox, which originated in Tahiti, was sweeping the Pacific. One of his Kanaka crewmen died of the disease. The log for August 11 states tersely: "Sank him and all his clothes."

Two more men were left ashore at Mazatlan, also suffering from smallpox. At that port, 32 soldiers, an officer, his wife and three children were taken aboard. The September 13 log entry reads: "Died on board the commanding officer of the expedition,

Don Jose Maria Sarmiento, having been sick all the passage."
The others were landed at San Francisco, where sailmakers went
to work on the schooner.

At the end of that year, 1842, Alvarado's term as governor
expired. He was replaced by Manuel Micheltorena, for whom
Cooper continued to sail. He was back and forth between Sausalito and Monterey, delivering provisions from Vallejo to Micheltorena, among other assignments, and running up further
"expenses" of $2,754. In December, 1843, he took a cargo to
Mazatlan, which included 127 casks of brandy, 23 barrels of wine,
six barrels of an inferior brandy called pisco, a barrel of olives, a
can of dried fruit, 16 hams, and 112 cheeses. Among his passengers were Larkin, Jose Abrego, Andres Pico, and a Captain
Wolter, all of whom returned with him as far as San Pedro in
February, 1844.

Cooper's log ends abruptly March 8 on the way to Monterey.
There was smallpox again among his Kanaka crew. John Swan,
also one of the crew, said that Cooper was ordered out to sea by
the governor on account of the smallpox, but replied that he
would see the governor damned first.

In May the schooner carried a Captain Flores to Mazatlan and
returned in June. In July, she arrived in Acapulco, where she was
driven ashore by gale winds on September 25.

The log, owned by the National Trust for Historic Preservation, and now held at the Bancroft Library, University of California at Berkeley, is sometimes a little difficult to decipher, but
excerpts from it produce the following picture:

A heavy storm in mid-July had buffeted the ship, the carpenter
finding places in the sides where the oakum was nearly gone
from the seams. New bolts were needed on the starboard side for
the main shrouds. Throughout the rest of July and August, the
carpenter was working constantly on repairs. By mid-September
squalls, rain, and gales were severe enough to prevent any small
boat from being launched and sent ashore.

At 3 a.m. on September 25, the schooner was almost dragged

onto the rocks despite three anchors. It was saved temporarily by a shift in the wind, but at about 4 a.m., the main chain parted and the *California* was driven onto the sandy beach at Acapulco, the "playa larga," where the sea broke completely over it.

Two days earlier the American corvette, the *Levant*, had arrived with Captain Page, who now attempted to come to Cooper's rescue. The spars were taken down to lighten the vessel. In constant rain and fresh south gales, everyone from the schooner went ashore in the *Levant's* boat and tried to help refloat the schooner, to no avail.

People on shore were employed to assist, but again without result. By the third day, however, some water casks were fastened outside the vessel in an attempt to raise her, and the lower mast was taken out, "always keeping a taut strain on the two anchors endeavoring to haul off shore. Had about 150 men on luffs but nothing would work. In night tide vessel worked ahead, took out 'foremast."

September 29. Vessel still onshore commencing to make water, at times rolling considerable. Cloudy and rainy.

September 30. At about 6, tide being quite high owing to the fresh gale, vessel began to move some ... the swell at 7 off the beach after being 6 days with constant strain heaving day and night ... With upwards of 3,000 weight of anchor attached to the vessel and at times over 200 men working on windlass, tackles, etc., at 4 p.m. moored again further towards Tambuco (?) than before... Could not examine the vessel much to find out the amount of damage.

From then until October 12, the crew worked at replacing and re-stepping the masts and getting the damaged rigging and stays repaired and replaced. The carpenter appears to have labored day and night. The log stops abruptly at this point and is not resumed until March 3, 1845, when Cooper notes that "at afternoon got under way from Acapulco after laying here since July 20th all hands excepting one man sick, some nearly 4 months, which is the cause of log not being kept—sickness owing to constant exposure to sun, rain, etc., while vessel on shore."

Despite further gales, rain, and high seas, the *California* survived its leaks and reached Mazatlan in 37 days, bound for San

Blas. Meanwhile, Cooper's family had no idea what had happened to him. On March 22, 1945, Larkin finally wrote to John Parrott, U.S. consul at Mazatlan:

I have waited many months for the arrival of my brother Cooper, master of the schooner *California* for Acapulco to return via Mazatlan in 3 months. Last September his schooner from her anchorage went ashore. The Captain was four months sick. Last February he was expected to sail.

When Larkin wrote the foregoing, he did not know that Cooper had finally left Mazatlan in April. The log of the *California*, which Cooper brought back to Monterey, explains the reason why he returned there on the schooner *Julia*, "having been compelled to leave the *California* for want of means to subsist, as the government denies having means to support the vessel, much less repair her. Therefore, my only recourse was to embrace the first opportunity in returning to California and about 2 hours before the vessel sailed the tesorario paid me 200 dollars of which over 100 dollars I gave the crew."

On May 7, 1845, the *Julia* got under way from San Blas to Monterey and on May 20 Cooper made his last entry in this part of the log: "Battering winds and sea...at 12 midnight dreamed an awful dream that all the teeth came out of my head."

2

FROM ALDERNEY TO BOSTON
TO THE SANDWICH ISLANDS

WHO, then was this Juan Bautista Rogers Cooper?
Where did he hail from?
What was his background and his reputation?
His precise birth date is unknown.

But on September 11, 1791, the parish church of St. Anne's, on the English Channel island of Alderney, registered the baptism of John Rogers Cooper, infant son of ship's captain Thomas Cooper and his wife Anne Rogers. The record was in French, then the official language of Alderney, just nine miles from the shore of France.

John Rogers Cooper was the only child of this marriage. His father, who came from Christchurch, Hampshire, England, was lost at sea with his ship when the boy was quite young. Again, the exact date is unknown.

In fact, there are still several missing pages in the story of John Rogers Cooper, later known as Juan Bautista Rogers Cooper, or by his nickname, Don Juan El Manco (One-Armed John).

He was, by turn, British, American, Mexican, and again American, by nationality. At some time during his youth he was attacked with a knife. The nerves of his left arm were cut, leaving him with a partly useless left hand. Thus his name.

He, too, was to become a ship's captain, sailing from Boston around the Horn, to Hawaii, to Canton, China, to California, to the Northwest, to Mexico, to South America, repeatedly.

Though his younger half-brother, Thomas Oliver Larkin, the first and only U.S. Consul to Mexican California, was to become much better known historically, Juan Bautista Rogers Cooper has long deserved at least equal attention as one of the most astute, versatile and influential men in California, from his arrival in 1823 to his death in 1872. He was an international trader, wealthy landowner—though perennially short of cash—and just as determined as Larkin that California should become a part of the United States, a goal towards which he worked incessantly, though always without fanfare.

Researchers have guessed that he was about nine years old when his widowed mother, Anne Rogers Cooper, brought him to Boston, Massachusetts, to join her sister, Martha Rogers, who had married another Captain Thomas Cooper, believed to have been a cousin of Anne's late husband. Martha Rogers Cooper had also been widowed, but the two sisters had a brother, Captain William Matticks Rogers, who made his headquarters at Dorchester, a fishing community on Boston Bay, and was a successful shipmaster in the East India trade, sailing also to China, the Sandwich Islands, and California as master of the *Hunter*.

"Uncle William" was to prove a strong support for Anne, Martha, and other members of the Rogers family, and a considerable influence in the life of John Rogers Cooper and other nephews. Martha had two sons: David, who later sailed as a mate on the *California* when his cousin John was commanding that ship, and another John Rogers Cooper (two cousins had the identical name), known as Sailor Jack.

Duplication of names has been just one of the problems facing researchers. A third Rogers sister, Mary Ellen Rogers Kittle, was born and died on Alderney, but sent her son, Samuel Matticks Ellen Kittle, to the United States in 1816 at the age of 10. Raised by his uncle, William Rogers, he adopted that uncle's name as his own upon entering the ministry and became pastor of the Congregational Central Church in Boston. He also handled financial affairs for his cousins who settled on the west coast and arranged schooling in the east for their sons.

Young John Rogers Cooper may have gone out to sea with the original William Matticks Rogers (Uncle William) after attending school in Charlestown. Furthermore, it is surmised that earlier this Captain Rogers could have brought John and his mother from Alderney to Boston during one of his voyages. In any case, there is a gap in the record of John R. Cooper between 1805 and 1819. In his possessions, after his death, was found the log of his uncle's ship, the *Hunter*, which indicates more than a casual interest in Captain Rogers' voyages. Also a drawing on the back of a map of India of some of the South Sea islands points to the likelihood that Cooper sailed there with his uncle and thus learned the seafaring trade.

Front and back pages are missing from the log, which covers the years 1810 and 1811. In April, 1811, the *Hunter* and two companion ships sighted an island listed as " southernmost in the Feegees." On July 3, the log stated, Captain Dorr of the *Bordeaux*, his first officer, and four of his best men "went up the country to fight a village and were all massercreed and three of them et." Despite this vivid description by Captain Rogers, Captain Dorr seems to have survived, since on July 8, crewmen from the *Bordeaux* and the *Brutus*, another ship which was in the vicinity, plus several hundred natives from other islands, attacked the cannibals' village once more, but in vain. Due to "treacherous business," as recorded in the log, the attackers were driven off, and all vessels left the bay. It would be interesting to know whether young Cooper had any part in this.

Boston, to which the *Hunter* returned, was at this time considered the hub of maritime world commerce, and the shipyards of Boston and Charlestown were turning out vessels as rapidly as shipwrights could build them. Massachusetts was the principal shipowning commonwealth in America. In 1806, more than 1,000 sailing ships entered Boston from foreign ports, and by 1830, the figure had grown to nearly 1,500. Between 1820 and 1830, the population of Boston grew from 43,000 to 61,000, and by 1842, it had passed the 100,000 mark.

There was one more shipmaster in the Rogers clan, John Weston Rogers, "Uncle John," who had eight children, six of them born either at Alderney or in England before he and his family came to Massachusetts, probably about 1808.

Still another sister, Lucy Weston Rogers, was married three times and had children by all three marriages, before arriving in this country sometime after 1813. Following the War of 1812, which the people of Massachusetts had strongly opposed, there was an influx of British to the Boston area.

On Nov. 29, 1801, the widowed Anne Rogers Cooper, John R's mother, married Thomas Oliver Larkin at Charlestown. One of their five children was Thomas Oliver Larkin Jr., always known as Oliver, who eventually settled in Monterey and became one of early California's most successful businessmen.

Of the other Larkin children, two died in infancy; a third, William M.R., died at age 17. A daughter, Anne Rogers Larkin Wright, always kept in touch and remained on the best of terms with her brother Oliver and their half brother, John Rogers Cooper.

Larkin Sr. died in Charlestown, April 18, 1808. Five and a half years later on Oct. 24, 1813, Anne Rogers Cooper Larkin married Amariah Childs, also of Charlestown, a widower with ten children. She and Childs had one son, George Edwin Childs.

One of the principal complaints of this considerable tribe of John Rogers Cooper's relatives was that they rarely knew where he was or what he was doing, as he seldom took the trouble to write to them. (There were so many of them, he probably couldn't keep track.)

The "practice account books" which he learned to keep at school in Charlestown, and which are dated 1804 and 1805, were valuable preparation for the precisely detailed accounts of all his transactions which he was to keep in the years to come, and to which he gave much more attention than to letters. These books are now on deposit in the Bancroft Library in Berkeley. Similarly,

Although this portrait was entitled Ann Rogers Cooper in a collection it is more likely Ann Rogers Larkin, daughter of Ann Rogers who married first Cooper, second Larkin, and third Childs. Ann Rogers, the mother, died in 1818 before photography was developed and the dress in the portrait is circa 1845.

Ann Rogers Larkin, the daughter, was a loving sister to both Cooper and Larkin, and wrote reports to them of their children after the latter went to school in the East. She married Otis Wright, had a family, but died fairly young in 1849, of tuberculosis (Society of California Pioneers).

the practice arithmetic books of his schoolmate and lifelong friend and business associate James Hunnewell, two years his junior, were a forerunner of the work which Hunnewell was to do as a ship's supercargo, trader, and merchant. These books are in the Baker Library at Harvard University.

According to Cooper's obituary, which was printed in the *Monterey Democrat* in February, 1872, he went to sea at the age of 14, in 1806. A "protection paper" issued to him by the Commonwealth of Massachusetts in 1808, a kind of passport for identification in foreign ports, describes a "large scar on the left arm, and nerves contracted of the left hand." A letter written by his half-brother, George E. Childs, in 1845, refers to the recent death of "Mr. Goddard, the same person who in his young day cut brother John's arm so badly." And a letter from James Hunnewell to Cooper in 1843 speaks of "that wretch Elisha Goddard that wounded you." These are the only clues to the injury which marked him for the rest of his life.

The records show that Uncle William M. Rogers, as master of the *Hunter*, was in Fiji and the South Pacific in 1810-11. But there is no indication as to whether young Cooper and his friend Hunnewell were part of the crew. On June 19, 1812, the United States declared war on Great Britain. What part Cooper, Hunnewell, or any of the Rogers family may have played in the War of 1812 is unknown. It was a war that was flatly opposed in maritime Massachusetts.

Uncle William retired to Charlestown during this period, American merchant shipping having fallen off badly due to various embargoes and blockades. It is known that James Hunnewell, unable to find a berth on any ship, went to work for a blacksmith, and young Cooper went to Brookfield and hired out to the Rev. Micah Stone, believed to have had both agricultural and industrial interests. Stone, a Harvard graduate, had married Sarah Ward of Charlestown.

A second "protection paper" for Cooper, dated January 8, 1816, repeated the description of his scarred left arm and described him as age 24, five feet five inches tall, with sandy hair and blue eyes. Apparently he was going to sea once more, but not with Uncle William, who, a widower for many years (his first wife drowned herself in Alderney), married a widow, Lydia Hersey, February 1, 1817.

A letter from George M. Larkin, one of Cooper's cousins, refers to a "long and tedious voyage to India" which Cooper probably made about this time, and expresses the hope that he will have better luck with his next captain, the one in question having been a Tartar. The ship returned to Boston in late 1818 or early 1819. In the meantime Cooper's mother, Anne Rogers Cooper Larkin Childs, had died, April 17, 1818 at age 47.

Of the half-brothers and sisters, Oliver Larkin was now almost 16, Anne R. Larkin was 13½, William M.R. Larkin, 11, and George E. Childs, 3½.

The George Larkin letter, typically, states that he has been expecting a communication (in vain) from Cooper, with reference to "the caprice, stupidity and meanness of a bad and unskillful captain," never identified.

Another letter from George Larkin to Cooper, dated October 11, 1819, refers to "your great aversion to letter writing," but acknowledges receipt of a note "although months have passed since you last addressed me ... [I am] happy to hear you have obtained so good a situation."

Cooper had signed as second mate on the brig *Thaddeus,* with Andrew Blanchard as master, James Hunnewell as supercargo, and a first mate named Spear.

October 23, 1819, the *Thaddeus* left the Long Wharf, Boston, for the Sandwich Islands (Hawaii), bearing the first group of American missionaries to establish themselves there. They were Congregationalists who had formed themselves into a Church of Christ at Park Street, Boston, and who were taking passage around the Horn to convert the heathen in the Pacific.

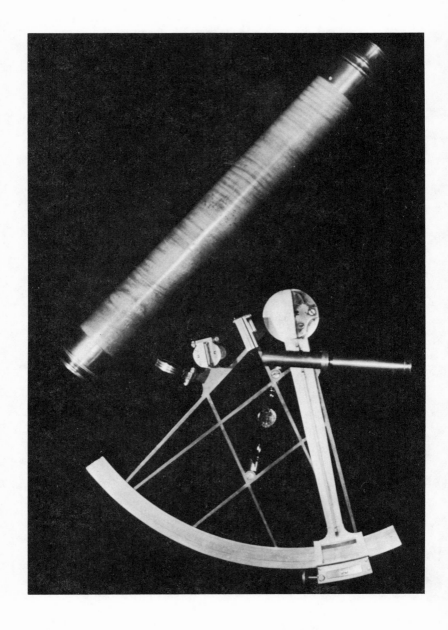

Sextant and telescope used by Cooper (Courtesy of the Pacific House Museum, Monterey).

3

A CARGO OF MISSIONARIES

THE American Board of Commissioners for Foreign
Missions had chartered the *Thaddeus* for $2,500, exclusive
of provisions, in order to send seven missionaries, their wives
and children, to the Sandwich Islands (so named by their discover-
er, Captain James Cook, in 1778, in honor of the Earl of
Sandwich.)

"You are to aim at nothing short of covering these Islands with
fruitful fields and pleasant dwellings, and schools and churches,"
the missionaries were charged, "raising up the whole people ... a
nation to be enlightened and renovated and added to the civilized
world."

The Rev. Hiram Bingham, a graduate of Andover Theological
School, was the leader of the group. Six days before sailing, he
had married Miss Sybil Moseley. With them were a Rev. and Mrs.
Asa Thurston; a physician and his wife, Dr. and Mrs. Thomas
Holman; teachers Mr. and Mrs. Samuel Whitney; Mr. and Mrs.
Samuel Ruggles; a farmer, Daniel Chamberlain, his wife and five
children; a printer, Elisha Loomis, and his wife; three Hawaiian
youths from the Foreign Mission School in Cornwall, Conn., and
a young Hawaiian chief, George P. Kaumauli; 23 in all. A second-
hand Ramage press was sent with them, so that Loomis, with a
few fonts of battered type, could print hymnals, catechisms, and
scripture tracts.

A cabin 20 feet long and 16 feet wide housed most of this
assemblage for the next five months. According to Albertine
Loomis (Elisha's great-granddaughter) in *Grapes of Canaan:
Hawaii 1820*, which was published by the Hawaiian Mission

17

Children's Society, the *Thaddeus* was skittish, wet, and noisome, with live chickens, ducks, and hogs in coops and pens on the deck. "Spars, ropes, chains, barrels, and a longboat left scant room on the quarterdeck ... those whose bunks were in the cabin might have slept in the marketplace, for all the peace and privacy they had. In rough seas, elaborate contraptions of straps, ropes, and boards were rigged to keep them from falling out of the berths. In fine weather the men bathed in the ocean. The women did not."

Chests and trunks were piled almost to the cabin ceiling. A semi-circular table lit by a swaying, smoking lamp, served for meals, meetings, and study.

In the journal that he kept, Daniel Chamberlain noted that "The first mate, Mr. Spear, is a violent opposer of religion, ridicules sacred things, and treats the name of Jesus with contempt. Mr. Cooper, the second mate, has been more thoughtful for some time past than usual—this circumstance seems to excite the enmity of Mr. Spear—calls Mr. Cooper crazy."

Cooper, in fact, became more sympathetic to the mission band as the voyage continued. The four Sandwich Islanders had previously sailed from their homeland to China, then around the Cape of Good Hope and across the Atlantic to New York or Boston. Rounding the Horn may have completed their nautical education, but Cooper was well aware that a winter passage through the Straits of Magellan was not exactly what anyone would have chosen. On March 29, 1821, the Islands were sighted.

After the tip of the Big Island (Hawaii) had been passed, a boat was sent ashore, manned by Hunnewell, the supercargo, and two of the islanders, Hopu and Honolii. They learned that Kamehameha, the first chieftain to rule all the islands, had died 10 months earlier, and had been succeeded by his son Liholiho.

The missionaries, it was said later, had arrived at the psychological time, "partially to offset the demoralization introduced by Boston traders and Nantucket whalers," to quote Samuel Eliot Morrison's *Maritime History of Massachusetts*. The whalers were just beginning to use the Islands as a base. It was estimated that by 1830 there were some 500 British and American vessels in the Pacific, and Honolulu was their logical port for refitting and obtaining provisions. Later in the 1830's there were more American vessels trading and whaling in the Pacific than those of any other nationality.

Hawaii, in fact, was becoming "as Yankee as New Bedford," with Massachusetts merchants established there and carrying on trade with California, Canton, Kamchatka and the smaller South Sea islands.

On April 4, 1820, 163 days out of Boston, the*Thaddeus* anchored off the village of Kailua, where King Liholiho and his queen were playing in the surf, along with hundreds of their subjects. Later in the day the king and his court were given dinner on the brig's quarterdeck.

Like his father, Kamehameha, Liholiho wanted to buy American ships. The payment was in sandalwood, then much in demand in Canton, China. Whereas Kamehameha had been a conservationist, restricting the cutting of the trees, Liholiho had stripped the hillsides. Boston traders had brought rum, brandy, champagne, clothes, furniture, carriages and all kinds of boats to stimulate the trade, again according to Morrison.

Captain Blanchard of the*Thaddeus* apparently had instructions from the owners, Hall and Thatcher of Boston, to sell the brig for sandalwood.

First, however, he wanted to visit the American west coast and to reach the fur ports of Oregon before it was too late in the season to obtain sea otter pelts, then bringing $35 each in Canton. He sailed from Kauai on May 2, 1820, having left the supercargo, Hunnewell, to set up shop in Honolulu with the help of five casks of rum and assorted merchandise. Hunnewell was to be responsible for the eventual sale of the*Thaddeus*, but was also commissioned to supervise the building of a schooner from materials sent out from Boston.

As supercargo, he was an agent for the owners in the sale of the cargo and in further purchases. He was to become one of the best known agents in Honolulu, but the sale of the *Thaddeus* and of a schooner, the *Little Thaddeus*, was to prove a thorn in his side for several years, even after he had his own ship, the *Tsar*.

By September 23, 1820, Captain Hale of the brig *Ann* had informed the missionaries that he had been in company with the *Thaddeus* on the northwest coast for several weeks, but that the *Thaddeus* had suffered some damage from striking a rock and had lost part of her false keel. In discharging the cargo, Hale said, a barrel of oil had been found belonging to the mission. "We are free from having such an accident laid to our charge (by infidels and scoffers)," was the comment of the missionaries, who made a note to remind Captain Blanchard that he had not fulfilled his contract in landing all the property belonging to the mission.

Cooper, however, seems not to have been included among the "infidels and scoffers," as the *Journal of the Sandwich Island Missions*, by Bingham, Thurston, Loomis, et al, had observed that, "We are happy to see that Mr. Cooper, the officer who for some time has appeared to be awake to the concerns of his soul, gives some evidence of an important change in his feeling. He has been a man of violent passions, which he had too often indulged in the most profane language, but his external reformation is very apparent and his conversation agreeable, and instead of his former unhappy condition of 'having no hope, and without God in the world,' his mind seems to rest in the pleasing confidence that in the all sufficient Saviour, even he may find pardon..."

On October 23, 1820, the *Thaddeus* and the ship *Volunteer* returned to the Islands from the northwest coast. On November 3, the missionaries received from the former vessel a load of bricks which had apparently been overlooked previously, and which was intended to supply the material for ovens and fireplaces. Two days later, Captain Blanchard and three of his officers attended public worship at the mission.

In a folder in the James Hunnewell collection in Baker Library, Harvard Business School, is a paper covering the sale of the

Thaddeus and *Little Thaddeus*, plus certain cargo and "appurtenances." Dated January 21, 1821, it specifies that Governor Boki of the island of Oahu will pay to "Andres" Blanchard, 4000 piculs of merchantable sandalwood. Witnesses to the agreement were John Sutes [Suter?], John R. Cooper; and James Hunnewell. A "picul" equals 133-1/3 pounds.

Ten days later, the missionaries were complaining that a variety of their articles brought out on the brig had not yet been delivered to them. Two days after that, they acknowledged receipt of one of their thermometers. On May 1, they objected that nearly half of the joists and some of the studs for one of their buildings were missing, several of the boards having been used by Blanchard during the passage from Boston. Though he had promised to bring them lumber from the coast, he had not yet done so, they said.

In July the *Thaddeus*, now Hawaiian owned, took a cargo of salt to Kamchatka with William M. Sumner as captain. It returned November 5 with a cargo of cordage, canvas, axes, and dried fish. Also in July, John Coffin Jones Jr., agent for Boston's Marshall and Wildes, and also U.S. agent for commerce and seamen, who had arrived in the Sandwich Islands in April, wrote from the village of "Hannarorah" to Marshall and Wildes: "The Islands are not what they were two years ago; they are glutted with every merchandise, and vessels more than they know what to do with ... Captain Blanchard and Cooper take passage to China in the *Alexander*, he leaves Mr. Hunnewell behind to collect the wood."

Collecting that sandalwood was to take a long time.

The previous November, Cooper's step-brother Ebenezer L. Childs, had written to him from Boston, chiding him for being remiss in corresponding:

"More than half of your time for the last 15 years has been spent abroad," Childs wrote. "You have traversed more than half the globe ... Captain John (Rogers) has gone on a voyage to the West Indies, [Uncle] William went with him ... Another of your cousins from England arrived some time since. Her name is Cooper [Lucy]."

It was nearly a year later that Blanchard wrote to Hunnewell from Canton, China: "Mr. Cooper is here and goes with me in the *Alert*, Captain Nye." They were on their way back to Boston.

Any details of the Blanchard-Cooper voyage to Canton have not yet been discovered. They arrived in Charlestown about March 25, 1822.

Meanwhile Hunnewell had written to Blanchard about the problems of getting the sandalwood shipped from Kauai. He did not hesitate to tell Blanchard that the latter's reputation in the Islands for sharp dealing had not helped. "Your character here is such that it has rendered my situation unpleasant and has exposed me and all concerned in the *Thaddeus* to frequent insults."

Hunnewell was to remain in Honolulu until 1824, trying to collect the wood promised as payment. For two years the *Thaddeus* lay, a dismantled hulk, and the Island chiefs became less and less willing to pay. Hunnewell referred to them as "mild tempered villains." Each picul of sandalwood was worth approximately $10 American, so $40,000 was at stake.

On the world scene, Mexico declared its independence from Spain, February 24, 1821. And California swore allegiance to Mexico, April 11, 1822.

Both events were to mean much in the life of John Rogers Cooper, who in 1822 left Boston again as master of the *Rover*, bound for California via the Hawaiian Islands.

And his friend Hunnewell's frustrations in trying to pressure the Hawaiians to produce the payment for the *Thaddeus* were just a precursor of Cooper's own experience when he eventually sold the *Rover* to California's Mexican government.

4

THE LOG OF THE ROVER

ON his voyages with Captain Andrew Blanchard to Hawaii, to the Northwest Coast, and to China, John Rogers Cooper must have made some money. Ship's officers were permitted to do their own wheeling and dealing in the ports they visited, and presumably Cooper realized a fair sum on the goods he brought back to Boston.

June 1, 1822, a certificate of clearance was issued for the schooner *Rover*, and a certificate of health for seven officers and men. The owners were listed as Nathaniel Dorr and William Blanchard of Roxbury and John R. Cooper of Boston. The amount of Cooper's investment is not known, but the cost of the schooner, including "apparel," was stated to be $7,509, and the cargo, victuals, etc., $9,313, for a total of $16,822. The *Rover* had been built in 1820 in Wiscasset, Maine. She was 62 feet 2 inches long, 18 feet 2½ inches wide, and 8 feet 6½ inches deep, of approximately 84 tons, with a square stern, no galleries, no figurehead, two guns, and a mixed cargo of merchandise.

Two days later, Cooper took personally on board: "one cambrick muslin gown; one suit of boy's cloaths; one gross of small buttons; one pair of silk shoes, lady's; four jack knives; one lady's capp; and one lott of ... [something undecipherable]."

June 5, the *Rover* set sail from Boston for Hawaii, the beginning of a "frightful voyage," since rounding the Horn required two months and the ship had been almost seven months at sea when it reached Hawaii on December 23.

At Fanning Island, south of Hawaii in the present Gilbert and Ellice Islands, and just north of the equator, a colony of adventurers was trying to establish a settlement but was having a hard time of it. John C. Jones, U.S. Consular agent in Honolulu, had been trying to send provisions to them but could not find a ship. He had told his employers, Marshall and Wildes, that he considered this "a losing business," but by February 5, 1823, he had persuaded John R. Cooper to make the trip on the *Rover* with the expectation of reaping a harvest of beche-de-mer, a sea cucumber much coveted in the Orient as an ingredient in soups.

Cooper was at Fanning Island on February 27 and back in Honolulu March 19. He must not have considered the beche-de-mer trade very promising, as he had made up his mind to sail next to California. Don Francisco de Paula Marin, a Spaniard who had become interpreter, royal physician, and distiller for Kamehameha I, and was probably the most influential European in the Hawaiian Islands in the early 1820s, wrote a letter of introduction for Cooper to Governor Don Luis Antonio Arguello of California, and on May 9, the *Rover* left Honolulu for San Francisco.

Marin had also had ideas of moving to California and buying a ranch, but a letter from Governor Arguello, dated July 17, 1823, at Monterey, informed him that there were no ranches for sale. "Futhermore," wrote Arguello, "by no means can I approve of your bringing four [Hawaiian] wives that are not legitimate, as I am informed that you have, and consequently some 20 children of theirs."

May 28 the *Rover* arrived at San Francisco. June 9, a receipt was given to Cooper for duties paid on his cargo. Three days later he was at Santa Cruz and the next day at Monterey.

Having no government ship to maintain contact with Mexico, Governor Arguello agreed to purchase the *Rover* almost as soon as he had seen her in Monterey Bay. The bill of sale, however, was not drawn up until the following December, 1823, and in the meantime, Cooper returned to Honolulu with a cargo of horses and cows. New Englanders had settled in Hawaii and had started this trade in California horses and cattle, which brought high prices in the Islands.

The animals were shipped either in the hold or on deck, boxed in by wooden frames, tied in slings, and covered with blankets to prevent chafing. Ample supplies of food and water had to be taken with them. The traffic was supposedly illegal, since Mexican law prohibited the exportation of animals, but the law was ignored, and by the late 1820s some 500 horses were known to have been shipped. The Hawaiians were soon "described as being second only to the Gaucho in equestrian skills." Cooper is said to have given the young chiefs lessons in riding.

One of his mates was Nathan Spear, a former Boston druggist's clerk (not the first mate of the *Thaddeus*). Spear, along with many other crewmen, had been desperately ill during the *Rover*'s voyage from Boston round the Horn and on its seven-month struggle to reach Hawaii. He had been carried ashore "so nearly dead as to be insensible," according to the files of the California Historical Society. It took Spear six months to regain his health, so when the *Rover* returned to Hawaii with the horses and cows, he decided to go back to Boston. But, in 1832, he was in California, having decided to open a store in Monterey.

Two cows and calves from the *Rover* were sold to the missionaries for $120, and one horse for $100. Some of the original cargo from Boston had been sold to Governor Arguello, but most of the rest was sold in Honolulu. It consisted of molasses, gin, brandy, rum, soap, shoes, canvas, "ship cloathes," caps, prints, muslin, shirtings, bonnets, crockery, cables and cordage, hardware, bread, "naval stores" and tobacco, plus 3,000 feet of lumber, two "chaldrons" of sea coal, and 10 quarter casks of wine.

The log of the *Rover*, preserved by Cooper's granddaughter, Frances Molera, traces his further travels, but without any written comment from him. As his step-brother, Ebenezer L. Childs, told him: "You must acknowledge yourself as lamentably deficient in performance of all epistolatory duties ... I really do not believe that there is a letter of three lines extant in your hand writing."

August 17, 1823, the *Rover* left Honolulu with missionary mail to be forwarded from California if he (Cooper) can find "a conveyance to America." His principal purpose in returning to Monterey was to deliver his ship to its purchaser, Arguello.

It may have been at about this time that "the waltz was introduced in California ... by some gay blades who arrived on the schooner *Rover* and, finding the fandango and jota not to their liking, taught the senoritas to dance the waltz," to quote from a letter in Gleason's *Beloved Sister*, a series written from California and the Sandwich Islands.

December 1, 1823, Governor Arguello signed a contract for sea otter hunting by the Russians at Fort Ross, who were given permission to bring 25 baidarkas for ottering in San Francisco Bay.

Despite his reputation for never writing a letter if he could help it, Cooper sent one on December 24 to his old friend James Hunnewell: "Old Hunnewell, Dear Boy ... in hopes to see you in about 50 days ... I feel easy on one acct. I have at last received the pay for the schr. in seal skins ... I have agreed to stay by the vessel one voyage or 7 months and then return home."

Notes from the typescript of seafarer Stephen Reynolds' Journal in the Peabody Museum in Salem show that early in 1824, a Russian brig from Monterey gave intelligence that "Cooper was taking a cargo of skins to carry to Canton for the Spaniards who bo't the *Rover*, will be here [Honolulu] very soon ... "

"Sunday, February 29, a sail came in sight, which proved to be the *Rover*. Cooper, 21 days from California—four horses, six heifers ... "

"March 1, Cooper landed his animals. Rode a white mare bro't for Navarro," Reynolds continued.

"Monday, 15, Schr. *Rover*, Cooper, went out and afternoon sailed for Canton."

Before leaving, Cooper had given Hunnewell a receipt for all the accounts and sales which the latter had handled for the owners, "plus $27 cash his balance due."

The *Rover* was not headed immediately for Canton, but sailed first for Fanning Island, presumably with additional provisions for the colonists there, then went to Manila, where among other business, including selling some otter skins, Cooper bought medical supplies. It was June 8, 1824, when he reached Canton.

A few days before that Hunnewell had written: "My hope of realizing something handsome from the *Thaddeus* has vanished.

"I have collected 28 piculs of the 4,000 ... 2,800 are lost in fire and expenses."

Cooper had seen the rotting hulk of the brig on the beach, where the purchasers could also view it.

His cargo for Canton included 303 sea otter skins and 300 tails, and 1,310 sealskins. The Russians had brought their baidarkas and Aleut hunters to San Pablo Bay, then to Monterey Bay, where in the first two months of operation they had brought in 429 skins. Among wealthy Chinese, the pelt of the sea otter was the most luxurious obtainable, coveted especially for mandarins' robes, ladies' capes, belts, sashes, hats and mittens, and for trimming on silk gowns.

When Cooper arrived in Canton, it was still, so far as foreign commerce was concerned, a near-monopoly for the British East India Co. By 1836, 12 years in the future, there would still be only 44 Americans and 28 Portuguese in business there, as compared to 162 British.

Passengers on the *Rover*, possibly sent by Arguello to supervise the handling of the cargo, were Santiago Estrada and Marcelino Escobar of Monterey. Procedure, however, was cut and dried for Westerners, who were required to hire a pilot at Macao and then proceed 30 miles up the Pearl River to the Whampoa anchorage.

Carl L. Crossman's *The China Trade* describes the routine Cooper had to follow. At Whampoa, a comprador was engaged to supply the ship with food. Taxes were paid and "cumshaw," or bribes. The captain and supercargo then proceeded to Canton ten miles up the river, where Chinese merchants had been given licenses by the emperor to conduct trade with "foreign devils" along a quarter-mile strip of river frontage.

These merchants had set up a "Co-Hong," through which a visitor had to sell, and purchase new cargo.

Favorite purchases, for both California and New England customers, were decorated trunks made of painted leather over camphorwood, in nests, four or five to the set, intended for clothing storage, especially in adobe houses which did not have closets. Fine carved chairs, rosewood tables, sewing boxes on stands with carved and lacquered legs, floor carpets, window shades, draperies, and other standard household decorations were imported to America in massive quantities, along with sofas, couches, silverware, ivory carvings, fans, paintings, porcelain, teas, and silks. Cooper brought back a complete set of table silver for a member of the Vallejo family.

His cargo for the Chinese may have included ginseng, a root found in the New England woods, called jen shen in the Orient and believed to have great medicinal properties; the aforementioned beche-de-mer from Fanning Island, and sandalwood from Hawaii.

(His uncle, Captain Rogers, had been in Canton as early as 1813, but whether Cooper was with him at the time has not been established.)

The sandalwood trade was fast dwindling in 1824. Though the fine-grained, fragrant wood had long been popular in China, it was becoming a glut on the market and was also increasingly difficult to harvest in Hawaii, partly due to fighting, which had broken out among the chiefs on Kauai, and partly due to the fact that the hillsides were rapidly being stripped. Hunnewell continued to attempt to collect the piculs still due Cooper, but it was a slow and frustrating task. By the mid-1830s sandalwood was all but extinct in the Islands.

There was a rumor current, circulated by a certain Captain Newell, that Cooper's co-owners had failed in business and that he had run off with their ship. Cooper told Hunnewell, wryly, to

Ivory carvings found at Cooper-Molera adobe. (Photos by Ralph Buchsbaum.)

thank Newell for him, if he saw him. Hunnewell, though, was preparing to head back to Boston temporarily. He turned over his Honolulu affairs to Stephen Reynolds, who had sailed to the Northwest Coast, Hawaii, and China as early as 1810-1813, had settled in Hawaii; and had become its leading legal adviser, unofficial and self-taught.

By October 23, 1824, Cooper was back at Bodega Bay, where the Russians could help him get the *Rover* overhauled and give him the latest news on otter skins. Arguello had made a new contract with them, and the Aleuts were hunting as far south as San Pedro. Cooper was to pick up the skins taken in the vicinity of San Francisco as part of the fur cargo on his next China voyage, but was not satisfied with the Mexican "quota" which the Russians were delivering.

It was January, 1825, when he arrived in Monterey and took on additional skins and tails, for a total of 444 skins and 263 tails, when he sailed once more on March 23. Because of a complicated system of collecting what was due him for the sale of the ship, it was to be a long time before the pay he received in sealskins could be translated into cash.

The government in Mexico City had sent word to Arguello that it did not have the means to provide for the needs of Lower (Baja) or Upper (Alta) California, which would have to depend upon their own resources. But to lighten this blow, a decree had been issued by which the port of Monterey was opened to foreign commerce, and San Francisco, Santa Barbara, and San Diego were declared ports at which "vessels of the Mexican nation might engage in coasting trade."

Since Mexico had almost no vessels in California waters until Arguello bought the *Rover*, and since the California ports mentioned, and the Franciscan missions, were already doing as much trading as they could promote with foreign vessels, the decree was about as useless as could be imagined.

Arguello's primary concern was how to pay his soldiers, who had long received scanty rations and no money. The missions, having been cut off from the "Pious Fund" which was supposed to be sent from their superiors in Mexico City to aid their endeavors, had long learned to be self-sufficient.

But Cooper's voyage to Canton for Arguello, followed by one more, gave hope in Monterey, at least, that better days were in store for California commerce.

It had been Arguello's idea that the *Rover* should also be used to carry correspondence between Monterey and the ports of San Blas and Mazatlan. But while Cooper was returning from this second trip to Canton, Arguello was replaced as governor by Jose Maria Echeandia, who was sent north by the republic as governor of the two Californias in November, 1825. Echeandia did not endear himself to the Monterenos by choosing San Diego as his capital.

In early 1826, Monterey's population was estimated at 114 civilians, plus the army.

In July of that year, Cooper sailed the *Rover* to Santa Barbara and then to San Diego. His agreement with Arguello had included permission to trade on his own account in Canton and to invest the money he received for the otter skins in "effects" for the California troops, who were poorly clad, among other deficiencies. Most of the effects were delivered to the "habilitado" of San Diego, but Cooper and Arguello got into an argument as to Cooper's share of the Canton sales.

Cooper wanted a board of arbitration to settle his claim on Arguello. The manner of the ship's nationalization was ordered investigated and the sale to Arguello confirmed, but the arbitrators also decided the case in Cooper's favor, in the sum of $5,000. "Which," Cooper wrote, "the damned rascal Arguello will never pay while California remains in its present condition."

Renamed the *San Rafael*, the former *Rover* was sent with a cargo to San Blas, with Jose Cardenas as captain. Mexican authorities there, unhappy at the idea of California having a vessel of its own, would not allow the *San Rafael* to return.

Captain John R. Cooper, a man without a ship, went back to Monterey to start a new phase of his career.

Encarnacion Vallejo de Cooper, born in Monterey, March 24, 1809, daughter of Ignacio Vallejo, "sargento distinguido" of the Spanish forces in Monterey. Ignacio and his wife Maria Antonia Lugo had 13 children, most of whom became prominent in California history. Encarnacion married Captain J.B.R. Cooper in Monterey, August 24, 1827. She remained Spanish-speaking throughout her life, devoting her time to her family and to her church. She died January 15, 1902, in San Francisco. (From oil portrait by California artist Narjot, with permission of present owner.)

5

COOPER MARRIES; AND COMES
TO THE AID OF JEDEDIAH SMITH

BETWEEN voyages, whenever he was in Monterey, Cooper lodged with Ignacio Vallejo and his family. Vallejo, of Castilian ancestry, had come up from San Diego in 1774 as a member of the military establishment at the Monterey Presidio, and like many other Presidio soldiers, had probably obtained a grant of a town lot where he built a house for his wife, Maria Antonia Lugo, and their 13 children. Here Cooper found a room and here he returned after relinquishing command of the *Rover*.

Best known of the children were Mariano Guadalupe Vallejo, who was to become military governor of Alta California; Corp. Jose de Jesus Vallejo, whose shore battery had temporarily held off the attack of the Argentine freebooter, Hippolyte de Bouchard, in 1818; Prudenciana Vallejo, who married Jose Amesti, wealthy Spanish-Basque ranchero and alcalde of Monterey; Josefa, married three times and mother of future Governor Juan B. Alvarado; Rosalia, who became the wife of Jacob P. Leese, prominent American merchant, and Maria Geronima Encarnacion Vallejo, who married Cooper, 36, at age 18.

Having spent more than 18 years at sea, Cooper had decided to settle down on shore and open a general merchandise store. (Its exact location is still not established.) His friend James Hunnewell had just returned to Hawaii to set up a store in Honolulu. Other merchants in Hawaii were starting a concerted drive to get China goods for sale in California, and Francisco de Paula Marin, who had written the letter of introduction to Governor Arguello for Cooper, wanted to know if Chinese merchandise was in demand in California, and what kinds he could supply, cheaper than other dealers. "Also give me their current prices," he asked.

(Though Arguello, replaced as governor in November 1825, had frowned on Marin's idea of buying a California ranch and bringing his Hawaiian wives and numerous children there, Marcelino Escobar wrote from the Monterey Presidio in January 1826, telling Marin that Don Mariano Castro would sell him a ranch.)

A dual personality, with a love both of the sea and of the land, Cooper was to spend the rest of his life building up a trading and land-holding empire which eventually stretched from Sonoma County to Big Sur. But after California came under Mexican rule in 1822, the permanent residence of "foreigners" was frowned upon, especially in the capital city of Monterey. In 1829 a naturalization law was passed by the Mexican Congress requiring all such foreign residents "to become Roman Catholics, to prove two continuous years of residence in the country, to have a useful trade or occupation, to renounce allegiance to other nations, and to swear to support the constitution and laws of the Mexican Republic."

April 14, 1827, Cooper was baptized as "Juan Bautista Rogers Cooper" at San Carlos Church, Monterey, with William E. P. Hartnell, the English trader who had become interpreter and translator for the Mexican government, as "padrino," or sponsor. That same year, on August 24, 1827, Cooper married Encarnación Vallejo. Almost nothing is known of their romance or betrothal, other than that Cooper had once written to Hunnewell telling of the difficulty of finding lodging in Monterey, of his being accepted as a boarder at the Vallejo home, "and there I met a long-spliced girl ... got to like her and married her ... I put it down as one thing done right in my life."

Like other early merchants up and down the California Coast, Cooper was soon engaged in the hide and tallow trade. The ranches and the missions were raising thousands of head of cattle which were slaughtered at certain times of the year, the fat boiled in huge kettles and the rendered tallow packed for use in candles and soap, and the hides soaked in sea water and then dried and shipped to New England to be manufactured into boots and shoes. For a time the British firm of McCullough, Hartnell and Company, operating under contract with Mexican authorities, had almost a monopoly on the hide trade, but there was room for entrepreneurs such as Cooper to supply the ships sailing to South America and Boston. Since there was little cash money in evidence, and most trade was by barter, hides became the currency of the time and were known as "California bank notes" or "leather dollars."

Though he was baptized and married in 1827, Cooper did not become a naturalized Mexican citizen until 1830. He was still feuding with the government over the sale of the *Rover*, but in order to own property he almost had to be a Mexican national.

According to W.W. Robinson's *Land in California*, the Mexican governors were given authority to grant vacant lands to "contractors, families or private persons, whether Mexicans or foreigners, who may ask for them for the purpose of cultivating and inhabiting them." Mexican nationals were given preference, and the governor used his own judgment in the case of the others. It was said that the prospect of obtaining land grants influenced many foreigners to seek naturalization, though a number of those who did so, including Cooper, supported the American cause in California for many years prior to 1846, when Commodore John Drake Sloat raised the American flag over the Monterey Custom house.

Within a year of going into business in Monterey, Cooper had to come to the assistance of the first of the "mountain men" to enter California from the east—Jedediah Smith.

Smith's Southwest Expedition of 1826 had as its purpose the exploration of the country lying southwest of the Great Salt Lake, to determine whether a Buenaventura River existed which would lead to the Pacific Coast, and to hunt for beaver. With 15 men he traveled down the Virgin and Colorado Rivers, crossed the Mojave Desert, followed the Mojave River to its source in the San Bernadino Mountains, arrived at the San Gabriel Mission and wrote to Governor Echeandia in San Diego, requesting horses, and permission to pass through the country, up to the Bay of San Francisco.

Echeandia was very suspicious that Smith had come on a military mission, even though shipmasters in San Diego harbor vouched for Smith's motives and the authenticity of his papers. Echeandia, nevertheless, ordered him out of California. Smith crossed the San Bernardino Mountains, the Antelope Valley and the Tehachapis, worked his way up the San Joaquin Valley and, by April 1827, was on the American River with 1,500 pounds of beaver skins, which he wanted to carry across the Sierra en route back to Salt Lake.

Mission heads and military authorities were alike alarmed at his presence. Fr. Narciso Duran at San Jose, president of all the missions, wrote to Ignacio Martinez, comandante at San Francisco, saying that the Smith party was stirring up trouble.

Smith, now on the Stanislaus River, wrote to Duran to explain that he was waiting for snow to melt, in order to cross the Sierra. The letter was forwarded to Martinez, who in turn sent it to Echeandia, who had moved to Monterey. Echeandia ordered Martinez to inform Smith that he must either leave the country, come to San Jose and await orders from Mexico City, or take a ship to Oregon.

Smith had other ideas. With two of his men, Silas Gobel and Robert Evans, he crossed the Sierra in eight days—the first time it had ever been crossed by white men—reached Salt Lake, living on horse flesh, then on July 3 arrived at Bear Lake for a rendezvous with trappers and with his partners, David Jackson and William L. Sublette.

Reoutfitted with supplies for two years, and with 18 men to accompany him, Smith set out for California once more, intending to pick up the men he had left on the Stanislaus and then trap his way up the California and Oregon coasts to the Columbia River.

Attacked by Mojave Indians while crossing the Colorado,

Smith lost half his party, but made his way via Cajon Pass and the San Bernardino Valley to Mission San Gabriel again. Thence he marched north and reached the camp on the Stanislaus on September 18. From there he rode with three men to Mission San Jose to try his luck with the recalcitrant Fr. Duran, but the latter showed no hospitality and, as before, referred the matter to Comandante Martinez after an American at Pueblo San Jose, William Welch, interceded for Smith.

When Martinez discovered that an Indian had given false information on Smith's plans, he ordered the Indian flogged, and heard Smith's plea that he be allowed to go to Monterey to see Echeandia. At this point Captain Cooper came from Monterey with Thomas B. Park, supercargo of the brig *Harbinger* from Boston, and stayed two days in San Jose to vouch for Smith, much to Jedediah's relief.

An "escort" of four soldiers had to be sent from Monterey, however, to bring Smith there. Upon his arrival he was locked up in the calabozo and treated as a United States spy, unwashed and unfed, until Cooper showed up the next morning with his breakfast. Jedediah was then taken to see the governor, who spoke only Spanish and sent for William Hartnell as interpreter. Hartnell was not available until later, so Smith was given the freedom of the town with Cooper as his host and escort.

Echeandia, at a later session with Smith, still could not believe that he had crossed the desert a second time without some ulterior motive, and wanted him shipped to Mexico City to state his case, with Smith paying his own way. This the explorer refused to do, even when Cooper offered him a loan. Finally Hartnell came up with a solution, whereby the masters of four American vessels then in the harbor could appoint a temporary consular agent. Cooper was appointed to the post and became responsible for Smith's good conduct.

The stubborn governor, though unwilling to make any move which might jeopardize his standing with the government in

Mexico City, nevertheless wanted Smith's party on the Stanislaus to come to Monterey. Smith objected that they were closer to San Francisco and finally received permission to send them there, after Smith and Cooper called on Echeandia on November 7 and gave him a written certificate. This stated the reasons for Smith coming to California and made Cooper responsible for the return of Jedediah and 17 men to Salt Lake. They were given a passport upon Smith's signing a bond for $30,000 guaranteeing faithful performance of the agreement.

Through Cooper, Smith also sent the United States minister to Mexico, a letter accounting for his presence in Mexican territory, and complaining of the harsh treatment he had received. He left with no very high opinion of Monterey.

Cooper had stuck his neck out for the Smith Southwest Expedition. In the years that followed, as one Mexican government succeeded another in California, and as England, France, Russia, and the United States all cast a covetous eye on that territory, there was never much doubt where Cooper's sympathies and support lay.

After the death of Smith at the hands of hostile Indians on the lower Cimarron in 1831, one of his partners, David Jackson, joined with the Tennessean master trapper, Ewing Young, and another frontiersman, David Waldo, to plan another expedition to California. Its purpose was also to trap beaver, and to take advantage of the expanding trade in horses and mules. Strong California mules in particular were in demand from Missouri as far as the flourishing Southern plantations.

Jackson was to go ahead and investigate the possibilities of this stock raising project, while Young and Waldo concentrated first on furs. Young gave Jackson a letter of introduction to J.B.R. Cooper, whom he had met on a previous trek from Taos, New Mexico, to the San Joaquin Valley and the California coast, and with whom he had become quite friendly.

In the Vallejo Collection of Documents at the Bancroft Library is a letter written from the "Red River" (Colorado) by Young to Cooper on October 10, 1830:

"Since I saw you in St. Joseph (San Jose) I have had my horses and mules stolen by the Indians. I followed them and recovered all but five of my best mules they killed to eat. We killed 10 or 12 of the Indians."

Unlike Jedediah Smith, Ewing Young had had the foresight to obtain a U.S. passport from Secretary of State Henry Clay, approved by the Mexican minister to the United States, and further gained the blessing of Fr. Narciso Duran at Mission San Jose when he pursued and captured some recalcitrant Indians with whom the mission had had trouble.

In the letter of introduction to Cooper which Young wrote for Jackson, he asked for assistance in the mule business and told Cooper that he, Young, planned to be in California in March 1832, and to return the following summer with some 30 or 35 men, intending to settle permanently. In his band of adventurers were Kit Carson and the latter's elder brother, Moses.

"I think it is likely we can make some further arrangements about the establishment above San Francisco," Young wrote further. Exactly what this meant can only be guessed at.

On February 28, 1832, Jackson wrote to Cooper from San Miguel Mission, saying that he was having great difficulty crossing the flooded river. The letter was addressed to "Don Whon Cooper." In Jackson's party was Job Dye, who later signed the agreement to raise mules on Cooper's Rancho El Sur.

When Young arrived at San Gabriel Mission, he was persuaded by Fr. Jose Bernardo Sanchez that there was an excellent opportunity in the sea otter trade, and decided to try his hand at collecting otter furs. In 1834 he wrote from somewhere on the Colorado to Abel Stearns in Los Angeles that he planned to erect a sawmill in California. Since Stearns was representing Cooper's trading business, and since Cooper had built a sawmill or two, this may have been a suggestion that they should join forces.

In August of that year, Young drove a large herd of horses and mules to Oregon after visiting Monterey.

What Young did not discover until he arrived in the Willamette Valley, was that Gov. Jose Figueroa of California had sent a letter by ship to John McLaughlin for the Hudson's Bay Company at Fort Vancouver, accusing Young and his men of being horse thieves. This Young indignantly denied to McLaughlin's face, but after he and his men settled in the Chehalem Valley, on the banks of the Willamette, it took years to straighten out relations with the Hudson's Bay Company settlers across the river.

On March 1, 1837, Young was back in Monterey, looking for a herd of cattle to drive to Oregon. Job Dye was to assist him. Young visited Jacob Leese at Yerba Buena and Mariano Vallejo at Sonoma, with Vallejo signing an order for the administrator of the missions to sell Young 1,000 head, including 500 from San Jose. Whether Cooper took an active part in this transaction is not known, but since he was constantly raising cattle at El Sur and moving herds to other ranches, it seems more than likely that some of the herd on the Oregon drive had been his.

(Leese had been in trade in Santa Fe in 1830 and met Young there, before coming to California in 1833 and to Monterey in 1836.)

Despite attacks by Indians and violent quarrels among his men, Young was successful in getting the bulk of the cattle to the Chehalem. From then on, a constant stream of livestock flowed from California to the Oregon settlements.

Young became the wealthiest American in the region, with a lumber mill, a grist mill, a trading post, a general store and bank, plus vast fields of wheat. He even sent to Hawaii for natives to work for him. "He and his colony of frontiersmen constituted the farthest outpost of American settlement," according to Kenneth L. Holmes, in his book, *Ewing Young, Master Trapper*.

And in all of this, Cooper, as Young's earliest California friend, had had a hand.

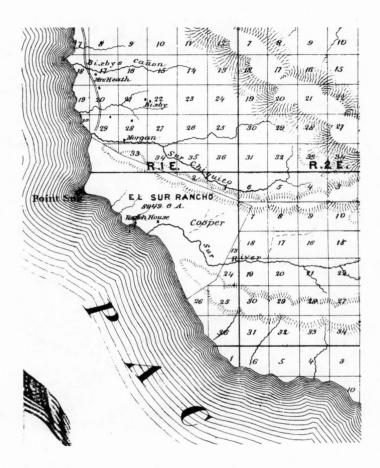

Map showing boundaries of Cooper's Rancho El Sur. The map was drawn when his son, John B. Henry Cooper, was chairman of the Monterey County Board of Supervisors.

Thomas Oliver Larkin, half-brother of J.B.R. Cooper, joined the latter in California in 1832, as clerk-assistant, but later struck out on his own, became one of the leading businessmen of Monterey, and was named U.S. Consul during the Mexican period. (Colton Hall Museum.)

6

MUSICAL CHAIRS
IN THE GOVERNOR'S OFFICE

AFTER his marriage, Cooper probably continued to live at the home of his father-in-law, Ignacio Vallejo, but petitioned the town council and received a grant of a town lot. He added to it later by purchasing a strip of land in the rear from Gabriel de la Torre, and much later another strip on the northeast side from San Rafael Estrada, son of Mariano Estrada. Among the several structures built on the Cooper property was a long story-and-a-half adobe, erected in 1832, part of which is now the Cooper-Molera adobe.

In this house, after the death of his granddaughter, were found magazines from England dealing with animal husbandry and dating to the early 1800s. Already he had ideas of developing his own herds. (This granddaughter, Frances Molera, received an "A" in animal husbandry in correspondence courses which she took through the University of California at Berkeley.)

His first move into the cattle business came in April 1828 when he rented the Bolsa del Pajaro rancho (site of present-day Watsonville) from Sebastian Rodriguez. From that date until the end of 1829, the rent was $30. For 1830 and 1831, it was $25. During this time Cooper built corrals, a barn, a small grist mill, and a house for eight ranch hands.

Cooper's deal with Rodriguez provided that when the latter quit the military service—he was sergeant in the Presidial company—Cooper would turn back the land and his improvements on it. This happened in 1832. Meanwhile, on high land near what is now Watsonville's main street, Cooper had used boards split from redwood at Corralitos to put up the buildings aforementioned. He had also entered into the lumber business through cutting redwood on Jose Amesti's rancho.

On December 29, 1828, the first of six Cooper children was born. She was Ana Maria de Guadalupe Cooper, usually known as Anita. On March 22, 1829, Cooper petitioned Echeandia for naturalization, which was granted May 29, 1830. He needed to be established legally as a landowner in order to have the wherewithal to raise a family.

In 1829 he bought 7,000 acres of the ranch known as Bolsa del Potrero y Moro Cojo (Pocket of the Pasture and the Lame Moor) and also as La Sagrada Familia (the Holy Family) from Jose Joaquin de la Torre, to whom it had originally been granted. It lay between the Salinas River and the Tembladera Slough, near present Castroville. Today the Molera road runs through it and extends to Nashua Road, and Mulligan's Hill lies within its boundaries. This was the first of the land purchases which were eventually to bring a fortune to Cooper's descendants.

He added to it the small portion now known as Mulligan's Hill after de la Torre had granted it to his compadre Juan Maria Mulligan in payment of a debt. Cooper bought it from the Mulligan estate, of which William Hartnell was the executor.

On Sept. 4, 1830, Cooper's second child, a son, Juan Bautista Henry Cooper, (always called John) was born. Cooper's family was growing and he needed money. He may have overextended himself financially, for in October 1833, he sold half of his Monterey house to John C. Jones, who sailed back and forth frequently between Hawaii and California.

Cooper needed a clerk-assistant to aid with the store and to keep his books. He wrote to Boston, offering the job to a stepbrother, Samuel Chapin Childs, son of Amariah Childs by his first wife, Ruth Larkin. Samuel, then in his early 20s, declined the offer, though he was to seek his fortune in California in 1849. A copy of Cooper's letter was forwarded to Thomas Oliver Larkin, half-brother to Cooper and step-brother to Childs.

Larkin was in North Carolina, having spent 10 years in the

South, as store and sawmill owner, justice of the peace for Dublin County, and postmaster at Rockfish. Plagued by ill health, he had not been notably successful in any of these ventures, so returned to Boston, sailed on the *Newcastle* for California, and reached Monterey on April 13, 1832, by way of Cape Horn, the Sandwich Islands, and San Francisco. He went to work immediately, straightening out Cooper's accounts. When Larkin arrived, he was accompanied by a lady, Rachel Hobson Holmes, whom he had met on the ship which brought him to Honolulu February 25, and thence to Monterey. She was the wife of a ship's captain, John Andrew Christian Holmes, but Larkin got her pregnant. Her husband fortunately died at sea March 8 on the brig *Catherine*, bound for Callao, and thus removed himself from the picture, though Rachel did not know of this until a letter arrived from Henry Virmond, dated July 16.

In 1954 a record was found at Our Lady of Sorrows Church, Santa Barbara, showing that the child which Larkin had fathered was baptised February 1, 1833, as Isabel Ana, having been born the previous day. She died in Santa Barbara at the age of five months.

The Coopers took in both Larkin and Rachel Holmes when they arrived in 1832, but there has been a question as to how the two half-brothers, Cooper and Larkin, got along, since Larkin left his employment with Cooper in February 1833, wanting to strike out for himself. It was obvious that Larkin saw opportunities beyond the Cooper domain, and though there was never any antagonism between the two, they were not intimate until later years, when family vicissitudes and tragedies drew them closer. Whenever the chips were down, the Larkins and the Coopers stuck together.

Whether or not Larkin could foresee himself as U.S. Consul at Monterey in the years ahead, he had refused to become a Mexican national. John Coffin Jones married Larkin and Rachel Holmes at sea on his ship, the *Volunteer*, off the Santa Barbara coast, June 10, 1833. She became the first "Senora Yanqui" to reside in

Anita Cooper, oldest daughter of Captain Cooper, born Anna Maria Guadalupe
Cooper, December 29, 1829. She was educated at home, and was written of as
one of the belles of Monterey during the days of the U.S. military government.
She married Herman Wohler, September 29, 1859, and they made their home
in San Francisco. Having no children, she devoted her life to her church and
close relatives. After her husband's death she lived with her widowed mother
and her sister's family—the Moleras. She died September 5, 1912, and was
buried in the Cooper family plot at Holy Cross Cemetery. (Society of California
Pioneers.)

John B. Henry Cooper, oldest son of Captain Cooper. Born in Monterey in 1830, he was sent to the missionary school in Honolulu and returned after several years to be educated by private tutors at home. After his father's death he managed the family holdings for some years and acquired more land, personally owning some 17,000 acres at one time. He served as a Monterey County supervisor and chairman of the board. Shortly after completing a fine new home on the Sur Ranch, he died there the evening of June 21, 1899, leaving his wife, three sons and one daughter. (Photo courtesy of Martha Cooper Lang.)

This deseño, or sketch map, of Cooper's first ranch property, Bolsa del Potrero y Moro Cojo (Pocket of the Pasture and the Lame Moor), also known as La Sagrada Familia (the Holy Family), was presented to the U.S. Land Commission, with supporting documents, to prove his ownership. Of interest is the meandering route of the Salinas River to the Bay of Monterey. This river was formerly called the Rio de San Antonio. Also of interest is the

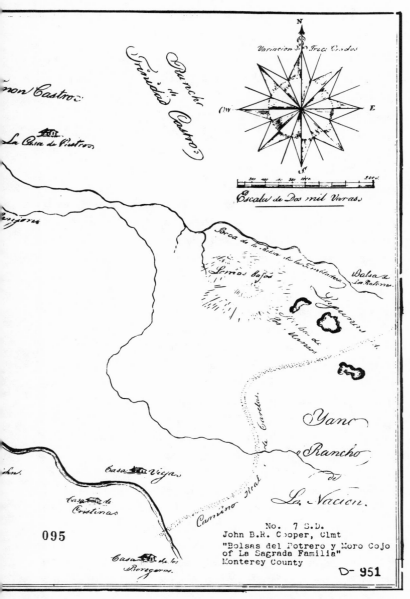

Rancho "Trinidad Castro"

non Castro:

La Casa de Piedros

N

Variacion 3 Trec: Grados

O

E

Escala de Dos mil Varas

Boca de la Bahia de la Trinidadera

Balsas las Ratones.

Lomos Bajos

Yeguario

Sierra de los Mosteros

Yano

Rancho de

La Nacion.

Casa Vieja.

Casa de Cristinas

No. 7 S.D.
John B.R. Cooper, Clmt
"Bolsas del Potrero y Moro Cojo
of La Sagrada Familia"
Monterey County

095

D- 951

Casa de los Borregeros.

old Camino Real de Carretas crossing the eastern part of the ranch. This route led from Monterey generally northward toward San Juan Bautista and communities in the San Francisco Bay area. Today Highway 1 and the branching Highway 156 toward Highway 101 are quite near the old route. Milligan's Head (or Hill) can still be seen rising above the artichoke fields. The sketch of Milligan's house marks the former ownership of part of the

California. All their children, however, were baptized into the Catholic faith, and Mrs. Larkin was baptized one day after a particularly difficult birth.

Cooper had also served as "guardian" for the lady involved in another runaway romance, Josefa Carrillo, daughter of Don Joaquin Carrillo of San Diego. She had fallen in love with an American, Henry Delano Fitch of New Bedford, Mass., who arrived in California in 1826 and in 1829 was baptized as Enrique Domingo Fitch. They were to have been married secretly with the bride's uncle, Domingo Carrillo, serving as the witness, but at the last moment he backed out, as did Padre Antonio Menendez, Dominican friar who was to have performed the ceremony. The fact that Governor Echeandia had had his eye on Josefa may have given these men second thoughts.

The bride suggested that Fitch carry her off. Her cousin, Pio Pico, took her on horseback to a boat, which was rowed out to a ship, the *Vulture*, where Fitch awaited her. Captain Barry, in command, was sailing for Valparaiso, where the lovers were married.

When they returned to California some time later, with an infant son, Fitch was master of the *Leonor*. He received a summons from Padre Sanchez at San Gabriel, sent Sanchez the marriage certificate from Valparaiso, but was ordered arrested in Monterey, where Mrs. Fitch was sent to Cooper's house. Her husband went to San Gabriel to state his case, but was held for trial. She petitioned Governor Echeandia to be allowed to join him.

Both were interrogated repeatedly by an ecclesiastical court, which finally decreed that Fitch should donate a bell of at least 50 pounds weight to the church in Los Angeles, that both should

ranch by John Milligan, an Irish sailor who came to California about 1814-15. (The spelling has since been corrupted to Mulligan). The Casa Vieja (old house) of the main rancho is depicted as standing near the cart route and the river. Cooper's ownership was confirmed by patent issued December 10, 1859, for 6,916 acres.

present themselves at church with lighted candles for three days of High Mass, and recite together for 30 days one third of the Rosary of the Holy Virgin, as penance.

As Cooper told Hunnewell, the one person with whom he corresponded regularly, "When I think of home ... I wish to God I was in Boston again ... for I have set my hat against these people [who] are trying every restriction on foreigners in this country to their own injury and ruining the trade here entirely ... may God prosper you in all your lawful undertakings."

It was about this time or a little later that Cooper's Aunt Lucy W. Connor wrote to him suggesting that this would "be a very good time to buy 50 dollars worth of new fashioned wigs ... as we understand your few straggling locks has disappeared ... hope you won't die a Roman Catholic."

Also his half-sister Ann Rogers Larkin wrote to him from Lynn, welcoming his wife to the family and wishing they would come and live in New England.

In Monterey, Cooper was known as a dependable, law-abiding substantial citizen who kept out of trouble but whose advice was often sought when it occurred.

In 1828 the soldiers at the Presidio revolted, after Echeandia had established his capital at San Diego. They were persuaded to return to their posts, but they rebelled again in November 1829, still half-starved and never knowing whether they would be paid. They found two leaders in the persons of an ex-soldier, ex-convict, and currently a ranchero, Joaquin Solis, and Jose Maria Herrera, the Mexican government's fiscal agent in California.

The rebels drew up a pronunciamento which Cooper and other foreigners listened to "out of courtesy," according to merchant David Spence. Solis then marched south with his followers and met Echeandia and his troops in a largely bloodless battle at Santa Barbara.

When Solis ran out of ammunition and provisions, he was forced to retreat, the principal casualty having been one horse. Echeandia caught up with the rebels in Monterey and had the leaders put in irons and shipped to Mexico. They were subsequently set free at San Blas.

Cooper, as he told Hunnewell in another letter, was having problems enough of his own without becoming involved in any political uproar. He was employing otter hunters, buying cattle, putting up ranch buildings, and finding that everything cost more than he had expected. Selling liquor apparently kept him solvent. "Most all kinds of licors sells except wines ... I have sold some years when here upwards of $10,000 of licor in a year."

Abel Stearns, who was to become one of the wealthiest men in the Los Angeles area, was now working as a traveling agent for Cooper's Monterey Trading Co., and Cooper in turn was aiding Stearns in the latter's business deals. Stearns was one of the foreigners who had joined with Cooper, Hartnell, Spence and others at Herrera's home to hear the Solis pronunciamento, but none of these men felt any urge to take political action until the role of governor assumed a "musical chairs" aspect.

Manuel Victoria was appointed to succeed Echeandia, but Echeandia refused to leave, won a minor battle against Victoria near Los Angeles, whereupon Victoria decided that he wanted to go back to Mexico. In January 1832, the provincial legislature elected Pio Pico civil governor. He resigned three weeks later when Echeandia refused to support him.

The British and Americans banded together in the Compania Extranjera to support Agustin Zamorano, who had been secretary to both Victoria and Echeandia. The Compania met at Cooper's house, elected Hartnell its leader, and resolved to oppose all revolutions. Its members disliked the vacillations of Echeandia and had no confidence in Pio Pico. They expressed willingness to act in defense of good order in the capital, so agreed to back Zamorano, who held office until Jose Figueroa was sent from Mexico in January, 1833.

Figueroa lifted trade restrictions and built up the business in hides and tallow. He died in 1835, however, and another series of governmental changes followed.

Though Cooper at one time may have had ideas of taking his wife back to New England, he was becoming too wrapped up in a diversity of California endeavors. John C. Jones, who had bought half the Cooper house so as to have a place to stay while traveling back and forth between Hawaii and Monterey, after three years sold it to Nathan Spear, who in turn sold it to Manuel Diaz. Cooper was cramped for space for his growing family, and also for members of his wife's family. Her father, old Sgt. Vallejo, died in 1832, and her mother moved in with the Coopers, who also had two of Encarnacion's sisters, Rosalia and Maria de Jesus, and Magdalena del Valle, a niece, aged 10, living with them until their marriages.

The Larkins, who had originally been staying with the Coopers, moved out to the Bolsa del Potrero Ranch for more than a year, where their first son, also named Thomas Oliver Larkin, was born. Then they rented half of the Hartnell house in Monterey. Hartnell had added two wings to the original one-story residence, which stood on the present site of the Monterey Peninsula Hospital. Hartnell by this time also owned the Alisal Rancho near Salinas.

Meanwhile Nathan Spear had come from Hawaii with his wife, Jane Holmes, in time to join the Compania Extranjera. Spear opened a store in Monterey and owned a schooner, the *Nicolas,* which he ran between there and Santa Cruz.

Spear, whose name appears frequently in commercial records of the time, formed a partnership with Jacob Leese and William S. Hinckley in 1838 to open a store in San Francisco, but split with them later in a quarrel over profits. He left his Monterey store in charge of William Warren. A nephew, William Heath Davis, Jr., later the author of *Seventy Five Years in California,* worked as Spear's clerk.

"The people I am acquainted with remain the same as usual," Cooper wrote at one point to Hunnewell, "but my wife she grows better every day, that is my opinion."

Grassy foothills, studded with oaks, are the typical cattle country of Rancho El Sur, seen here from the Old Coast Road.

In the crowded conditions in which she was living, she would have had to be a marvel. Added to all the other people who nearly burst the Cooper home at its seams, were the orphaned children of relations, who were passed around among aunts and uncles as a matter of course, until they could fend for themselves. Encarnacion's sister Josefa, married three times, died after having 14 children, who were parceled out thus, some of them with the Coopers.

The only thing as uncertain as the number who would sit down to a meal on any one day at the Cooper table, was the matter of who might be holding down the governor's chair in Monterey.

After the death of Governor Figueroa in 1835, Mariano Chico held office for three months, then became involved in a scandal which even the free and easy Monterenos would not tolerate. He showed up at a public function with his mistress and with another woman who was under arrest, charged with adultery. His fellow citizens became so enraged that Chico had to hide aboard a ship bound for Mexico.

Juan Bautista Alvarado, born in Monterey, and then a young man of 27, appeared as leader of a new revolutionary movement whch included Mexicans, Indians, and some Americans headed by Isaac Graham, who operated a distillery in the Pajaro Valley. Equipped with only one cannon ball which would fit his single piece of artillery, Alvarado managed to hit the house of the governor in Monterey. The opposing force, led by Nicolas Gutierrez, surrendered.

It was from Alvarado that Cooper was to obtain his most valuable and spectacular piece of land, the Rancho El Sur.

56 COOPER

Mariano Guadalupe Vallejo, brother of Encarnacion Vallejo de Cooper. Born in
Monterey in 1808, he entered the military service and ultimately became
military comandante of California during the Mexican period. The historian
Bancroft listed him as one of the most independent and powerful men in
California. He urged Captain Cooper, his brother-in-law, to acquire land grants
in the Sonoma and Marin County areas. Vallejo served in the first Constitu-
tional Convention and was elected to the first Senate of the State of California.
(Portrait courtesy of Martha Cooper Lang.)

7

MARIANO VALLEJO AND
JUAN B. ALVARADO

COOPER'S brother-in-law Mariano Vallejo was a cadet at the Monterey Presidio when they first met. As the son of Sgt. Ignacio Vallejo, Mariano was entitled to schooling at the Presidio and proved an outstanding pupil, one who embraced learning and had a passion for books. There were many persons of education in his family background, including a number of priests. Born in Monterey in 1808, he entered the military service in 1823 and rose steadily in that profession, becoming active comandante at Monterey.

In 1829 he was taken prisoner briefly by the Solis revolters, but made a name for himself that same year by leading a punitive expedition against rebellious Indians, and the following year was transferred to San Francisco, where he became comandante in 1831. As a member of the diputacion during the revolution against Victoria, and again during the Echeandia-Zamorano period, he was absent in the south much of the time, but in 1833 he was sent to the northern frontier of Alta California to inspect the Russian establishment at Fort Ross and select a site for a Mexican fort. The government in Mexico City was becoming alarmed at Russian advances down the coast, and began giving serious thought to military defenses.

Vallejo made an official report on what he had seen, and in his own mind must have decided that Mexico, if ever it was challenged, would have little chance of hanging onto California.

He saw to it that his foreign friends received land grants, among them Cooper. He was building up a bastion around himself.

In 1834 he was promoted to lieutenant and sent as comisionado to secularize the Solano Mission. He was also made grantee of the Petaluma Rancho and was entrusted with the preliminary steps towards establishing a civil government in San Francisco. In 1835 he was the founder of Sonoma and was made military commander and director of colonization on the northern frontier. Though sent on various campaigns against troublesome Indians, he managed to win their friendship to a large extent and employed many of them on his growing estate. There they earned a wage, something that the missions never paid them.

Vallejo was devoting himself to the development of the Frontera del Norte. It was said that whenever Mariano arrived in Monterey, however, there was an uproar of hugging and kissing and cheering by all his relations and friends. He was rapidly becoming known as one of the most powerful men in California.

Though he took no active part in the removal of Mariano Chico as governor, it was his nephew, Juan Bautista Alvarado, who succeeded Chico, and under Alvarado, Vallejo was named comandante general of California and was advanced to the rank of colonel.

There are those who have observed that Cooper was shrewdly looking to the future when he married into the Vallejo family, which was to become one of the foremost in the country.

But in 1827, when Cooper took Encarnacion to the altar, Mariano was a 19-year-old Presidio soldier with decidedly slim prospects, and his father, Ignacio, certainly had no wealth.

Encarnacion was one of the belles of the town, with several suitors, but Cooper, living in the Vallejo home when he was not at sea, apparently had the inside track. His friend Hunnewell, replying to Cooper's letter telling of his marriage, remarked that "You neglected to tell me how beautiful she is."

Otherwise, there is no detailed description of Encarnacion now extant, and the two portraits remaining show her when she was an old woman. She learned little English, and Cooper always wrote to her in Spanish. It is known that she was always a devout

Juan Bautista Alvarado, nephew of J.B.R. Cooper and of Mariano Vallejo, served as governor of Alta California from December, 1836, to December, 1842. It was from Alvarado that Cooper acquired the Rancho El Sur, trading lands in the Salinas Valley. (Colton Hall Museum.)

Catholic, passing her strong faith to her daughters and worrying that her sons, while at school, might lose their adherence to that faith.

The second son, Guadalupe Alfredo Guillermo Rogerio— known to the family as Rogerio—was born February 1, 1838. A second daughter, Guadalupe Francisca Amelia, was baptized March 30, 1844. She was known as Amelia. A third daughter,

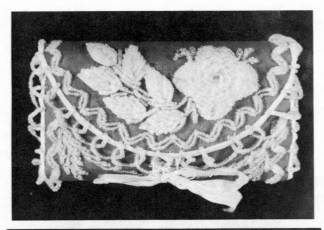

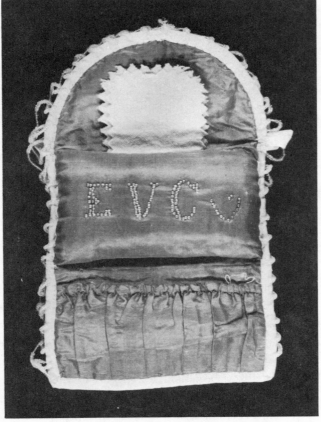

Sewing kit of Encarnacion, white beads on red velvet, exterior (Elkinton).
Sewing kit, interior, showing initials of tiny pin heads (Elkinton).

Amada Eloisa Guadalupe, was born June 1, 1846, but died shortly before her third birthday and was buried May 27, 1849. The third son, and last of the six children, was Jose de Jesus Guadalupe, called Guadalupe by the family and born March 13, 1848.

Cooper, as aforementioned, was chronically short of cash, though theoretically wealthy in terms of land.

In 1833 he petitioned for, and was granted by Governor Jose Figueroa in December of that year, a tract of two and a half square leagues in the Sacramento Valley known as "Rio Ojotska." The name was later changed to American River, probably because of the number of Americans who eventually established themselves there. Cooper, however, never settled there, deciding that travel between the ranch and Monterey was too inconvenient, though he added a second tract on the Ojotska to the first.

After Mariano Vallejo had made an official visit to Bodega and Fort Ross, he told Cooper of the productive region he had seen. That region, lying between the Estero Americano and the Russian River, was then inhabited by only a few Russians and Indians. Vallejo wanted to discourage the inroads of the Russians and Cooper decided that he wanted to trade his Rio Ojotska holdings for four square leagues at the junction of the Russian River (Sotoyme) and Mill (Mark West) Creek. He also suggested to Vallejo the names of three men, McIntosh, Dawson, and Black, whom he had known as sailors and who also wished to apply for grants. All four, including Cooper, were granted tracts in that Sonoma County area, by Governor Nicolas Gutierrez, who approved Cooper's trade of the Ojotska land.

Cooper called his tract El Molino, built a water-powered sawmill there, and a house of redwood lumber. He planned to stock the ranch with cattle.

In 1834 Governor Figueroa had granted a tract of 8,940 acres south of the Little Sur River to Juan B. Alvarado. Alvarado preferred the Bolsa del Potrero Rancho of his uncle, Cooper, and the two made a trade in 1840. (Alvarado's mother, Josefa Vallejo, was Encarnacion Vallejo Cooper's sister.)

Later, Cooper bought back the Bolsa del Potrero from Alvarado. John Swan, who visited there in 1845, described his experience as follows, in an article reprinted in April, 1934, in the *Salinas Daily Post*:

The Cooper ranch house was near the Estrada crossing, and the grist mill for grinding wheat by mule power stood close by. The mill and ranch were in charge of Bill Matthews, and from having charge of the mill, the native Californians called him Molinero—the miller ...

The old mill was moved to a knoll near the Tembladera. It was altered into a dwelling house. The previous winter, when the rains overflowed most of the lower plains, John B.H. Cooper had to be taken off the upper part of the adobe house in a boat, and as like most Californians, he disliked salt water, he got his father to have the mill moved, fearing they might have to take a cruise on it in Monterey Bay, by way of the Salinas River against his will.

In 1840 Cooper added to his holdings through a grant of 8,877 acres from Alvarado, in present Marin County. It was the Rancho Punta de Quentin, named for Chief Quentin, a notorius thief and daring Indian warrior, who was captured there. Later the name of the ranch became corrupted to "San Quentin," though no saint was connected with it. San Quentin Prison now stands on its eastern tip and San Anselmo at its northern edge. Ross is near its center.

Cooper put up three palizada dwellings on the site, in 1840, 1844, and 1847, also a frame dwelling in the late 1840s. He also leased a sawmill site to John Folsom of the U.S. Quartermaster Department, providing for the cutting of timber for the U.S. Army.

In 1844, Manuel Micheltorena, who succeeded Alvarado as governor, granted the Rancho Nicosia, also in Marin County, to Pablo de la Guerra and Juan B.R. Cooper. It consisted of 16 square leagues or 56,621 acres and was named for St. Nicasius. An earlier grantee was an Indian, Teodosio Quilaguegue, who received it from Governor Figueroa in 1835 but failed to "prove up" on it.

In all this buying and trading of land, Cooper was invariably hard pressed for cash, and found that construction expense, then as now, was considerably higher than he had figured. In 1836-37, Indians had raided his El Molino Ranch and killed or driven off half of his cattle. In 1838 a severe earthquake shook Monterey and interrupted commerce. When he looked at possible additions to his land empire, it was in terms of timber which he could turn into cash.

"I am so damned poor. I have got no money," Stephen Reynolds quoted him as saying repeatedly.

Faxon Dean Atherton, in his *California Diary 1836-39*, tells of being at Mission San Solano in December 1837, after having walked three miles over a muddy road with Cooper, the rain pouring in torrents.

"G-damn the rain," Atherton quotes Cooper as exclaiming. "It will be sure to carry away my mill dam then heigho for ruin. Thank God they are not so civilized in this country yet as to put poor debtors in prison. That's one consolation for me."

In March 1838, Cooper wrote to Abel Stearns, saying that his sawmill at El Molino had bankrupted him, owing to an incompetent millwright. Up to his ears in debt, he was going to the U.S., he said, to find a dependable man to run the mill. He asked Stearns to send him two shirts and a pair of trousers for the trip, as the pants he had "have more than four patches in the arse."

Many historians have credited Cooper with being the first commercial lumberman in California. In 1971 the site of his sawmill at El Molino was established as California Historical Landmark #835. "In addition to sawing redwood lumber, the mill and settlement served as a barrier to Russian encroachment from the west. Located ½ mile east on Mark West Creek, the water-powered mill was destroyed by flood in the winter of 1840-41," the official designation states.

Cooper's sawmill at Punta Quentin, which he leased to the U.S. Army for timber cutting, gave him further credentials to the title of "first commercial lumberman."

In later years Cooper's son John told historian Hubert Howe Bancroft that in 1838 "All my family went to visit my uncle

In 1834 J.B.R. Cooper constructed California's first known power-operated commercial sawmill on his El Molino Ranch in Sonoma County. In addition to sawing redwood lumber, the mill and settlement served as a barrier to Russian encroachment from the west. The water-powered mill was destroyed by floods in the winter of 1841-42, but on January 31, 1970, the site was declared California Historical Landmark No. 835. A plaque was placed there by the State Department of Parks and Recreation, in cooperation with the California Division of Forestry and the forest products industries of the state.

Salvador [Vallejo] and Mariano Vallejo in Sonoma and on the way we stopped at my aunt's, Mrs. Leese, at Yerba Buena. We started from Monterey in Spanish carts drawn by oxen and driven by Indians, with my grandmother, my aunt Mrs. J. Vallejo, my mother, brother, and sister. It took about two or three weeks. After staying a few days in Yerba Buena my uncle Salvador came from Sonoma in a launch to take us to Sonoma. Some Indians managed the boat. When we arrived in Sonoma we made up our minds to remain all winter."

Cooper did not go east that year, despite what he had written to Stearns. He was preparing to resume a seafaring career, and for the next 10 years, he was on shipboard as much as he was on land.

Thanks to Alvarado, Cooper was able to cope with most of the annoyances of dealing with the Mexican government. Though he liked the Mexican Californians in general, and they liked him, he was frequently in a temper over the officials sent from Mexico, over the constantly changing rules and regulations which made it difficult to do business, and over the almost constant even if bloodless revolutions prompted at first by far-away Mexico's rule and later by factional struggles between Northern and Southern politicos in California itself.

Atherton, in his *California Diary*, also tells of traveling with Cooper to Mission San Jose: "During the night [I] was continually annoyed by Cooper's damning the fleas, who as they would not let him sleep, appeared determined that no one else should, and between the two, I had but a small allowance."

As an employee at that time of Alpheus B. Thompson, a Santa Barbara merchant, Atherton's duties brought him into intimate contact with the administrators of the secularized missions, the native inhabitants, and the growing number of American settlers. His business activities involved him in the overthrow of Governors Mariano Chico and Nicolas Gutierrez, and the rise to power of Juan Bautista Alvarado.

In 1840 Alvarado quarreled with his former comrade-in-arms Isaac Graham, and fearing that the "foreigners" planned to take over the land, arrested many of them, with the exception of his uncle, Cooper, Abel Stearns in Los Angeles, and others who had married Mexican wives.

According to William Heath Davis in his *Seventy Five Years in California*, about 70 resident Americans were rounded up and shipped to San Blas on the Mexican bark *Joven Guipuzcoano*, accompanied by General Jose Castro. Prominent among them was the Kentuckian hunter, Graham.

News of this coup was sent to Washington by Thomas O. Larkin. As a result the U.S. sloop *St. Louis* was ordered to Monterey but arrived too late to be of service. Nathan Spear was among those arrested but was soon released. Davis was also held for 24 hours but had a great time at a dance at the home of the Yerba Buena alcalde, Don Francisco de Haro.

Eventually all prisoners were released at Tepic and were free to return to their homes in California. The Mexican government disclaimed all responsibility for the arrests and promised indemnification.

Sir George Simpson had no great opinion of the "slovenly habitations of San Francisco and Montery ... Santa Barbara, in most respects, being to Monterey what the parlor is to the kitchen," but, aboard the *Cowlitz,* he was able to observe that "The town [Monterey] occupies a very pretty plain, which slopes toward the north and terminates to the southward in a tolerably lofty ridge. It is a mere collection of buildings, scattered as loosely on the surface as if they were so many bullocks at pasture, so that the most expert surveyor could not possibly classify them even into crooked streets ... The dwellings, some of which attain the dignity of a second story, are all built of adobes, being sheltered on every side from the sun by overhanging eaves, while towards the rainy quarter of the southeast they enjoy the additional protection of boughs of trees, resting like so many ladders on the roof. The walls ... are remarkably thick, though this peculiarity is here partly intended to guard against the shocks of earthquakes, which are so frequent that 120 of them were felt during two successive months of last summer ... the shocks being seldom severe and often so slight, as to escape the notice of the unini-tiated stranger."

When William Heath Davis was in Monterey a year or two earlier, he had recorded that at that time there were in the town David Spence; Thomas O. Larkin, later U.S. Consul from 1844 to 1846; John B.R. Cooper; Major William Warren; James Watson, a grocer; George Kinloch; James Stokes, English merchant;

Edward T. Bale, physician, a native of England; William E.P. Hartnell, the Mexican government instructor and interpreter. "These were the prominent foreigners there. Among the Mexicans and Californians were Jose Abrego; Manuel Diaz; Don Antonio Maria Osio, collector of the port; Juan Malarin; Estevan Munras; Don Pablo de la Guerra, Rafael Gonzalez, Raphael Pinto [the last three connected with the Custom House]; also, Jacinto Rodriguez, Jose Amesti, Don Manuel Castro, Francisco Pacheco, who were engaged in stock raising; Mariano Soberanes; Jose Antonio Vallejo, also engaged in stock raising, a brother of General Vallejo; Manuel Jimeno and Dona Angustias his charming wife; Governor Juan B. Alvarado, General Jose Castro, Francisco Rico, Francisco Arce, and others."

To return to Sir George Simpson, who was traveling around the world in 19 months and 26 days:

"As to public buildings," he wrote of Monterey, "this capital of a province may, with a stretch of charity, be allowed to possess four.

"First is the church, part of which is going to decay, while another part of it is not yet finished. Its only peculiarity is that it is built, or rather half-built, of stone. Next comes the castle, consisting of a small house surrounded by a low wall, all of adobes. It commands the town and anchorage, if a garrison of five soldiers and a battery of eight or 10 rusty and honeycombed guns can be said to command anything. Third in order is the guardhouse, a paltry mud hut without windows. Fourth and last stands the custom-house, which is or rather promises to be, a small range of decent offices, for, though it has been building for five years, it is not yet finished.

"The neighborhood of the town is pleasingly diversified with hills, and offers abundant timber. The soil, though light and sandy, is certainly capable of cultivation, and yet there is neither field nor garden to be seen."

Simpson noted that Monterey was poorly supplied with water, "the small stream which runs through the town is generally dry in summer." He wrote of "the extraordinary drought of last year."

This, then, was the capital of Alta California, where the Alvarado-Vallejo administration ended on December 31, 1842. Manuel Micheltorena then became governor and in July of 1843 finally reached Monterey from Los Angeles, having put down a series of civil uprisings en route.

8

AT SCHOOL OVERSEAS

THROUGHOUT the latter part of the 1830s and most of the 1840s, Cooper's hardships, financial and otherwise, seem to have bothered him most in terms of his not being able to afford what he considered proper schooling for his sons.

He wrote to Larkin from San Diego: "Oh if I had any security of paying for Rogerio's schooling. It really makes me feel disagreeable and sick when I see the two little boys [Larkin's sons, Tommy, almost 12, and Frederick, 10] going where they can get their living when grown up, and I see my children the way they are. There is something that makes me feel as I do not do my duty."

Cooper was in San Diego, seeing the Larkin boys off on a voyage to the east coast, to school, and himself en route to Lima, Peru, to take a course in piloting. At age 55 he was almost an old man by the standards of the day, and knowing that he was no longer in physical shape to captain a vessel for long periods of time, he wanted to qualify to pilot ships in and out of California's anchorages. (In one of his earliest experiences as a pilot, in October 1838, coming from San Francisco on the schooner *Fearnought*, with Captain Dare, he had missed Monterey in the fog.) He matriculated successfully, but was still in Lima when Commodore John Drake Sloat, on July 7, 1846, landed at Monterey and annexed California and a vast western territory for the United States. It was Larkin who persuaded Sloat that he must take action and not dally any longer on his flagship in the bay, where he had arrived five days previously.

Cooper also missed the short-lived Bear Flag Revolt in Sonoma on June 14, when a group of settlers led by frontiersman

Ezekiel Merritt captured the semi-abandoned Mexican fort, arrested Vallejo, raised a home-made flag bearing a single star and a grizzly bear, and announced the formation of the California Republic.

Vallejo, who was in favor of the United States taking over California and bringing some stability to a vast area which received scant attention from a government in Mexico City, was far from pleased at being arrested and taken to Sutter's Fort to see John C. Fremont, who was said to be the guiding hand behind the revolt. This Fremont denied. Vallejo was released at about the time the revolt fell apart and Sloat moved in.

As soon as Cooper got back to California, he leased his San Quentin Rancho to Theodore Cordua so that the latter could raise vegetables and meat for whaling ships and U.S. warships.

It was on one of these warships that Cooper's eldest son, John, had been taken to school in Hawaii, according to John's own account to Bancroft.

The ship is identified in the records only as "U.S. frigate," and John Cooper told Bancroft that the date was 1841,though his arrival may have been a little later. Nine children in all went from Monterey to Hawaii, among them young Cooper, T.O. Larkin, Jr., Francis Watson, David Spence, Jr., Felipe Gomez, Henry Fitch, Jr., Romualdo Pacheco and George and Catharine Kinloch. Young Pacheco hailed from Santa Barbara and was the stepson of Captain John Wilson. They all attended the Oahu Charity School, established by the missionaries for the benefit of children of Hawaiian mothers and American seamen fathers. The advantage for the "foreigners" of Monterey was that their offspring could study English there, something that was impossible in Monterey, where the school language was Spanish.

Young Oliver Larkin traveled to school on the *Alicope*, Curtis Clapp, captain, and the sons of Messrs. Spence, Watson, Kinloch, Wilson, and Henry Fitch went on Captain Henry Paty's bark, the *Plymouth*. There is also reference in letters between teachers and parents to the *Levant*.

Two of the teachers in Honolulu, Andrew Johnstone and his wife Rebecca, broke away from the Charity School and founded their own seminary, to which the Monterey children transferred, along with another 21 students. A letter written by Mrs. Johnstone to Mrs. Larkin, March 25, 1844, speaks of John B.H. Cooper as "high tempered, obedient, and gives us no trouble." However, young Larkin, visited by his godfather, William Hartnell, in Honolulu, revealed that one weekend, he and his California friends had lassoed three natives, California style, and had to be bailed out of jail by the American consul to the Sandwich Islands.

In May, 1844, a letter from Stephen Reynolds to Larkin mentions the *California*, captained by Juan B.R. Cooper, having been in the islands, so presumably the latter visited his son at that time.

In December, 1843, Andrew Johnstone had written to Larkin:

With much satisfaction do I speak for a moment on the improvement of your relative, i.e. John Cooper, during the last 6 months. He is very diligent in school & progresses in the study of Geography, with great ease to himself. J. is very willing to be employed, & has occasionally assisted in hearing others. This plan we have found highly beneficial even to older scholars, as some naturally have not retentive memories.

You will have the kindness to communicate this information to your brother-in-law [he meant Cooper] and say to him that his son's expenses during the last year have been very trifling. Two prs of shoes & a hat are the only articles I now remember of purchasing. Mrs. Johnstone is having 4 prs of trowsers prepared for him at this moment. His health is perfectly good. I am a great while since hearing from Capt. Cooper!

Aug. 7, 1844, John Cooper wrote to his father:

I have another opportunity of writing you these few lines by the United States Ship *Warren*. I am very well, also Mr. and Mrs. Johnstone, and Oliver Larkin and Catharine Kinloch.

The king made a party on the first of August and they fired the canons and beat the drums and fifes.

The first party they made was for the white people and the chiefs. At the second and third parties that they made they didn't fire so many canons as the first, but the second party that they made they fired the canons in the night and

CORNELL'S

FIRST STEPS

IN

GEOGRAPHY.

BY

S. S. CORNELL,

CORRESPONDING MEMBER OF THE AMERICAN GEOGRAPHICAL AND STATISTICAL SOCIETY.

NEW YORK:
D. APPLETON & COMPANY, 346 & 348 BROADWAY.
CINCINNATI:
RICKEY, MALLORY & COMPANY.

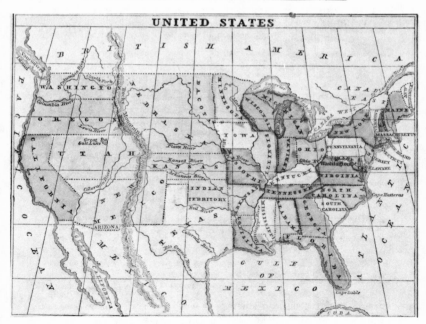

One of many school books found in Cooper's home.

beat the drums and fifes. When they were beating the drums and fifes I went to see the negroes dance.

Dear father I wish you to tell me when I am going to Monterey to see you and Mother.

Dates conflict in the several accounts of John's return. But Hartnell told Bancroft that "young Cooper remained there with the missionaries for two years ... there being in those days no school teaching English in California ... returning home in 1844, whereby he gained a familiar use of English although the more ready use and the accent of the Spanish mother tongue always marked his speech."

John B.H. Cooper in his own memoirs wrote that after his return from Honolulu he went to the school of John H. Rule, a Scot who came to California in 1847 from Callao and taught at Monterey. Meanwhile his younger brother Rogerio had been attending the Spanish-speaking school of Florencio Serrano in Monterey. (Serrano was one of the colonists who had come from Mexico with the Hijar-Padres expedition of 1834 on the *Natalie*. Cooper took a dim view of the expedition's leaders, believing that their aim was to take over the missions, which would have spoiled his business relationships there. In a letter to Abel Stearns, he referred to Hijar and Padres as "these rascals," but had nothing against Serrano, nor against Jose Abrego, who was another of the colonists and became a pillar of the Monterey community.)

John's school fees in Honolulu had been $100 per year. William French, a friend of his father, who had been keeping an eye on John, wrote to say that he had arranged for his voyage home in the brig *Peabody*, and asked that Cooper Sr. remit the balance due on his son's expenses, "in California soap"—$16.66 worth. French remarked that John "has made good progress in learning English, but requires a strict master."

When there was some talk of sending him east to school with Rogerio and the Larkin boys a few years later, John decided that he was too old to be a schoolboy any longer.

As to the benefits of having attended school in Hawaii, Felipe Gomez became Monterey postmaster, David Spence, Jr. followed in his father's footsteps as a successful businessman, Francis Watson became sheriff of Monterey County, Romualdo Pacheco became California state treasurer, then governor, then a member of the U.S. Congress; Catharine Kinloch married George W. Bird, member of a well-to-do Salinas family, and John B.H. Cooper became a Monterey County supervisor.

In November, 1846, Stephen Reynolds wrote from Honolulu to Larkin, Sr. "Tell John R. Cooper not to be too proud now he lives under what he has so long wanted—Stripes. I presume his landed estate will make him rich as a Nabob, so that he will leave ploughing the deep."

Captain Cooper, however, was far from being a wealthy man under U.S. rule, at least by his own estimate. Floods of the winter of 1841-42 had destroyed his Sonoma County sawmill. Supposedly he had been receiving $90 per month as captain of the *California*, but the Mexican government had owed him more than $5,000, dating back to 1826. On January 1, 1846, California's public debt to Cooper for services rendered was still $3,845, according to Larkin.

In October 1841, William Hartnell had been offered a chance to buy Fort Ross from the Russians. Unable to make the deal, he referred the opportunity to Cooper, who also could not afford it. In December of that year the Russians announced that they had sold the fort to John Sutter.

In November 1843, James Hunnewell wrote to Cooper from Boston to inform him that "upwards of $2,000 had been recovered from Blanchard and Dorr," who were co-owners with Cooper of the *Rover*, back in 1822. Cooper had had a claim outstanding against them for years, in settlement of his share of the profits. The settlement was a compromise by the arbitration board, and should have been much higher, Hunnewell said, "but your documents and accounts were so irregular."

It was Cooper's cousin, Samuel Kittle (who changed his name

to William Rogers and became pastor of the Central Church in Boston), who finally obtained the settlement.

In September 1844, subscribers were signing up at $100 each per year to establish a higher grade school in Monterey. Among them were Hartnell, Abrego, Watson, de la Guerra, Pio Pico, and Jimeno, but Cooper was not among them. He was shipwrecked at Acapulco, and for months after his return he was trying to pay medical bills. He was also being dunned to pay bills run up earlier in Honolulu.

Supposedly in 1845 he made a small fortune as one of the principal salvagers when the English schooner, *Star of the West*, was wrecked at Point Lobos. Three Californians were drowned during the salvage operation, which culminated with the wreckage and boats being auctioned off at less than $150, and from a cargo costing £25,000 in Liverpool, about $3,000 was realized at auction. There is a story, which has never been confirmed, that Cooper and his men brought ashore from the wreck packages wrapped in waterproofing, and rushed them through Customs at Monterey as "damaged goods," at half their value.

James Watson and James Stokes were the "disinterested" merchants who reportedly arbitrated the value at 50 per cent.

Would Cooper have resorted to such trickery? Or was it even considered trickery at a time when, according to Sir George Simpson, there were a dozen Mexican Customs officials in Monterey, each with his hand out, and it was thought to be a sport and challenge to outwit them? Also, was Cooper simply following the law of the sea?

In any case, what sort of a man was Cooper, according to his contemporaries?

He had served as a regidor, or councilman, for two years in Monterey, 1834-35, in charge of the city's public works and with investigating the cost of a new jail and city hall. He advised against the latter, saying that the city could not afford it, and recommended an unpretentious building for the jail.

William H. Thomes, who visited Monterey in 1843-45 on var-

ious vessels and later wrote a book, *On Land and Sea*, stated that
Cooper, "when on shore, dispensed a liberal hospitality to all
who were honored with his acquaintance, and who that traded on
the coast of California did not know him, and respect him? The
Captain was an elderly man, a thick, stout old fellow, nervous and
abrupt in his movements, and had a peculiar habit of biting one
of his hands—the one that was withered—when in a passion or
laboring under excitement. No matter who was near him, or
what he was saying, if suddenly vexed, up would go his hand to
his mouth, and he would take cruel nip at the member, and then
seemed satisfied that he had done his duty, and cool off."

W.D. Phelps, in his book published in 1871 under the title
Forward and Aft, spoke of the fact that Cooper:

> ... could not relinquish the sea altogether, and was placed by the (Mexican)
> government in command of their Navy, which consisted of an old schooner
> named the *California*, on which the Commodore hoisted his pennant when
> ordered to perform any naval duty.
>
> The old gentlemen is still living, and long may he survive, as he is a rather
> original character ... A seaman of the old school, he despised a long-tailed coat
> and would not discard a sailor's jacket. Known throughout California for his
> integrity and good nature, his honest countenance was always welcome wher-
> ever it appeared. The slouched white hat, blue short jacket, grey satinet pants
> and cowhide shoes constituted his every-day dress at all seasons from year to
> year and his uniform on all occasions.

Unable to obtain any government money to repair the *California*, Cooper had returned to Monterey but hated to give up the
sea, as Larkin remarked in a letter to Stephen Reynolds, when in
the late 1840s, he estimated his step-brother's worth at $100,000
"in land."

It was Larkin who gave him the opportunity to go back to the
sea for the last time.

9

COOPER'S LAST VOYAGE:
A PLACE FOR ROGERIO

C ALIFORNIA'S first newspaper, *The Californian*, launched in Monterey by Walter Colton and Robert Semple on August 15, 1846, and moved by Semple to San Francisco the following May, published the first note on the discovery of gold at Coloma, on the American River, in its edition of March 15, 1848.

John A. Sutter, at whose mill the discovery was made on January 19, 1848, had sent a sample of the gold to U.S. military Governor Richard Mason in February, but it was the end of May before Colton, Monterey's alcalde, entered the news in his diary. Governor Mason left Monterey on June 17 to visit the site, after which his account to the War Department created a sensation. "I have no hesitation in saying," he wrote, "that there is more gold in the country drained by the Sacramento and the San Joaquin Rivers, than will pay the costs of the late war in Mexico a hundred times over."

It was not long before both Monterey and San Francisco were depopulated of all able-bodied males, who had left for the diggings. Camps and tent cities were springing up overnight along the American River and its tributaries, on hillsides and in ravines, and the merchants selling supplies were prospering as fast or faster than the miners.

Among these merchants were Thomas Oliver Larkin and Jacob P. Leese of Monterey. Larkin owned a ranch on the Sacramento River in Colusa County which he called "The Children's Ranch," since under Mexican law he had not been able to own it in his own name. It was near enough to the gold country to serve as headquarters for his business with the mines, even though squatters were moving in from all sides. Juan B.R. Cooper had traded his ranch on the American River for his "El Molino" in Sonoma County, but drove cattle up to the American to sell meat to the miners.

Cooper's son, John B.H., reminiscing for historian H.H. Bancroft in later years, recalled that "In 1849, I went to the Molino Ranch in Sonoma owned by my father to get some Indians and horses to go to the mines. I bought four head of cattle, made jerk beef and started in company with others and the four Indians to work for me. I was to furnish the provisions and they were to work for me every day in the week excepting one which they were to work for their own benefit. The most I got out of them in a day was 20 ounces of gold. I spent almost everything in speculation. After leaving the mines I returned to my father's ranch in Sonoma to leave the Indians and take fresh horses to return to Monterey, and as it was very hard to get servants, I thought to speculate in Indians. The price to be paid was three blankets for each Indian."

Not everyone prospered in gold, but Larkin and Leese were able to pay $15,000 in gold dust for the brig *Eveline* on January 16, 1849. Leese was to be half owner and supercargo, and Juan B.R. Cooper was to be captain. The *Eveline*, built in Kennebunk, Maine, in 1839, was a two-master of 196 tons, 86 feet long, and was destined to repay the investors handsomely.

Cooper needed some good fortune. He had been involved in another shipwreck, that of the brig *Elizabeth*, at Santa Barbara, February 11, 1848. Captain Edward A. King was nominally in command and Cooper complained in a letter to Larkin that "I had the name of captain but had nothing to say on board the vessel." Larkin and David Carter of Boston were empowered by the owners of the *Elizabeth*, which had gone aground, to make the best disposition of the wreck and cargo. Cooper, sure that he would be blamed, was exonerated, but was given the responsibility for selling what was left of the brig, a time-consuming job which paid only his expenses. (Nevertheless, an exchange of letters between Cooper and King showed that they remained friends.)

The previous April, Larkin had placed on the market a town lot which Cooper owned in San Francisco, in order to raise $2,000 to pay Cooper's outstanding debts. The latter wanted a new command to get back on his feet financially.

On February 12, 1849, the *Eveline* was in Monterey with Cooper at the helm, and Larkin wrote to Stephen Reynolds in Honolulu, "My brother has $100,000 of land but will not sell. He prefers to go to sea."

Meanwhile, another Cooper, Thomas, grandson of the "other" Captain Thomas Cooper, Juan B.R.'s uncle, was en route to California from the East on the *Duxbury*, bringing with him a sailboat, which he intended to run between San Francisco and Sutter's Fort, carrying passengers. Or so cousin William Rogers informed Larkin.

The *Eveline* sailed from Monterey February 18, with a crew of nine, arrived at Honolulu March 12, and left there March 23 for Hong Kong. She had departed from Monterey, which the Reverend Samuel Willey, a February arrival on the steamship *California* (not to be confused with Cooper's schooner), described as "a land of quietness. One or two men are now and then seen walking the streets."

The town had not been as bereft of life since the summer of 1844, when 80 of its inhabitants were said to have died of smallpox.

July 1 the *Eveline* was in Hong Kong. December 29 she was back in San Francisco, bound for Monterey. It was estimated that each $500 invested had brought some $10,000 in return.

Invoices showed that Leese had sold 39 bags of his and Larkin's gold for $60,129. Among the items bought with the proceeds were jewelry, handkerchiefs, satin dresses, colored blankets, men's dressing gowns, rosewood writing desks, chests of drawers,

straw table mats, silk rebozos, Chinese lanterns, ginger, preserves, ivory, puzzles, and pictures, all of which found a ready
market among the men (and their wives) who had made money
in the mines.

How much Cooper may have invested is not known. This was
his last voyage, and in 1851 he was named Monterey harbormas-
ter. His return from Hong Kong was saddened by the news that
his youngest daughter, Amada Eloisa, born June 1, 1848, had died
in infancy and been buried at San Carlos Church, May 27, 1849.

Absent as he had frequently been for long periods of time, he
was nevertheless always concerned about the well-being of his
children. Once again, he began thinking of how Rogerio should
be sent to a proper school in the East. The only way, so far as he
could see, was to sell two of his ranches, Nicasio and Punta de
Quentin. For his share of the former, he obtained $10,000; for the
latter, $55,000. The buyer was B.R. Buckelew, who also owned
part of Rancho Nicasio. The sale was on October 25, 1850.

Several months earlier, on March 2, Cooper had decided that
he could take Rogerio to Boston. With the Larkins, they left
Monterey for Panama on the steamer *Oregon*, crossed the Isthmus, then took a ship again to New York. Larkin had traded his
Monterey house to his partner, Jacob Leese, for property in San
Francisco, but before moving there, intended to spend some time
in the East on business.

This was Cooper's first trip back to Boston in nearly 30 years,
but he had innumerable relatives there to make him feel at home
and to welcome Rogerio.

Cooper's cousin, William M. Rogers, the Congregational minister, was to be Rogerio's trustee. Cooper's half-sister, Ann Rogers, died May 21, 1849, and her husband Otis Wright, was to keep
an eye out for Rogerio's welfare. The three Larkin boys, Oliver,
16, Frederick, 14, and newly arrived Francis, 10, were to be his
schoolmates at a private school, Mr. Weld's, in Jamaica Plain, a
Boston suburb. Cooper could return to California with the assur-
ance that his son would be well taken care of.

Cousin William soon wrote to Cooper:

> Rogerio is well and happy. He bore the separation from you, better than I expected ... Mr. Weld gives me assurances that he will do well.

Young Oliver Larkin wrote to young John Cooper:

> I know your father was very glad to go back to California ... When Rogerio has been in this country about one year he will know English. Whenever he goes with me he always talks Spanish as in Monterey ... Rogerio and I want you to send us four Lazo [lassos], two for each of us. We want two made of horse hair or you know what kind to get. I have taken a common one and caught the boys and they look at me as if it was some great.

Young Frederick Larkin wrote to his cousin, John Cooper:

> Rogerio says that he likes Monterey better than this country, and he can't ride calfs here as in Monterey, as it is too hot here in summer and he all the time sees any piece of water, he wants to jump in. Our Master won't let us go into the water only when he is with us ... Mr. Weld has a pond on his land and when Mr. Weld aint home he goes in the pond but if Mr. Weld catches him he will whip him ... It is too hot for him in the summer and too cold in the winter.

By February of 1851, Cousin William reports to Cooper Sr. that Rogerio grows stout and tall, and needs new clothes. "He is a master at play, and his clothes suffer."

Rogerio, just 13, "writes quite well, reads English and Spanish tolerably, while he is behind in his Arithmatic [sic]," added cousin William. "He speaks English quite well. His studies are reading, writing, and arithmatic [sic], and the translation of Spanish into English. As soon as it is best, he well be put into Geography, Grammer [sic], etc."

At the end of that quarter, the Reverend Rogers proposed to place Rogerio under the care of a private tutor, LaFayette Burr, in Newport, R.I.:

> ... from no complaint of Mr. Weld's school, but from the belief that it will be for his advantage ... Rogerio is hearty and well. He is a noble-looking boy. He has improved, but in writing more than reading ... Say to his Mother I will allow no one to interfere with his religion, I mean, I will allow no one openly or covertly to assail his confidence in the R.C. faith. When he goes to Newport, he can attend the Catholic church there. But I object to our Catholic Schools, not because they are Catholic, but because they do not furnish as good an education as others.

Only Oliver, of the Larkin boys, attended the Newport school with Rogerio. Frederick and Francis attended day school in New York, where their parents had rented a house. But the unexpected death of the young minister, Reverend Rogers, from a stroke on August 11, 1851, complicated and confused the plans for Oliver and Rogerio. Alpheus Hardy, a business associate of the Reverend Rogers, and Uncle Otis Wright were to take over Rogerio's affairs, and Wright wrote to Cooper, Sr., saying that Rogerio wanted to return to the Weld school. It soon appeared, however, that both the boys were more interested in boating and fishing than in improving their minds, and were expecting and looking forward to John Cooper soon joining them, and bringing the bows and arrows and lassos that they had asked for. But John, at 21, felt too adult to return to schooling.

Whether it was the fact that Oliver and Rogerio were constantly getting into scrapes with a sailboat, or that he had only one other pupil at this point, Mr. Burr decided to "make other arrangements for another school," as Larkin wrote to Encarnacion Cooper. Whereupon Hardy and Wright determined that Rogerio ought to attend "a good school," Andover Boys' School, and so informed his father.

If Cousin William had still been alive and able to make the decision, Cooper Sr. might have agreed, but his concern for Rogerio's future persuaded him to set out once more for Boston, in a great rush. He deeded the Monterey home property to his wife, told his son John to consult with Monterey businessman David Jacks if necessary, and in May 1852, crossing the Isthmus of Panama on muleback, met his half-brother Larkin headed in the opposite direction, returning to California. In June, Cooper sailed for home again, having made a record round trip.

Rogerio soon wrote to him from Andover:

> I have to study very hard here. All I have to do is study all the time as hard as I can put in. I have to come up in my room at six o'clock and then I have to go to recite at half past ten and that takes all the morning till about twelve o'clock and then I come up to the house and don't have dinner till one o'clock and then I

have to go to recite and when I get thru about half past two o'clock I have to go
in the house and do my sums to the next day and I have to go without my dinner
but that is nothing. I wish John was here in Andover to school.I guess he would
have to stare round some. I like the school very and the teachers are very kind
and they are most all the time behind you and making the Boys study. I wish
when you write me a letter again and write to Mr. Hardy to get me a watch
because I want one to tell what time to go to school. Because the rool of the
school is if you do not come in at half past eight they turne the Boys out of the
school and I do not wish to get turned out of the school.

On October 1, 1852, Hardy wrote to Cooper:

Your son has continued at Andover and has done well. I am yet strongly of
the opinion that he is in the right place. He is well and happy so far as I can see.

On June 16, 1855, Cooper said in a letter to his old friend Abel
Stearns, "My boy Rogerio arrived here from the States a short
time ago well."

Rancho El Sur. A few of the more than 7,000 acres that still make it the most impressive stretch of Big Sur countryside. The view is from a point just off the Coast Highway, looking south.

10

MANAGING THE LAND

C OOPER loved the sea but he also loved the land, and one of his principal problems was to manage his properties when he was often away for several months at a time. He had to rely on others to act for him, or he leased out parts of the land on shares or a rental basis, giving the renter sufficient incentive to develop it.

As related earlier, Cooper obtained almost 7,000 acres of land along the lower part of the Salinas River by purchasing it in 1829 from the original grantee, Jose Joaquin de la Torre. This was and is fine soil producing excellent crops. Cooper placed some cattle on the land, but as the American farmers came into California in the 1850s he leased the land to individuals in plots ranging from 50 acres to several hundred. In 1869 in his personal account book he listed 36 lots in Salinas, totaling 6,422 acres, which were rentals. Among the renters were Michael O'Neill, E.J. Preston, J.H. Ashle, B.O. Walker, John W. Mellus, Edward Logwood, A. Copeland, Benjamin H. Drum, James McDonald, Reubin Jeffrey, F.D. Hall, etc. He also built a house for himself on the land where he and the family could stay. This was about a mile from what became Cooper's Switch on the railroad line leading to Salinas.

The second large rancho acquired in Monterey County by Cooper was a tract of almost 9,000 acres along the coast some miles south of Monterey, today known as the Big Sur area. This grant was originally made to Alvarado, then 25 years of age, of a prominent family, and soon destined to become a governor of California.

On Dec. 9, 1840, Cooper and Alvarado signed an agreement whereby Cooper gave to Alvarado his lands in the Salinas Valley, and Alvarado gave to Cooper the Rancho El Sur, extending from the mouth of the Little Sur River, on the north, to Cooper Point on the coast to the south. Andrew Molera State Park now lies on a part of this grant, as do the Naval Facility and the Point Sur lighthouse.

Three years later, however, Cooper bought back the Salinas lands from Alvarado for $1,000 in coin. Thus by December of 1843 Cooper had almost 16,000 acres of ranch lands in present day Monterey County. He is believed to have started developing the Sur land before the deed was signed, for as early as 1834 he signed a contract with Job Dye for the latter to raise mules for him there.

Dye was a Kentuckian who came to California originally in the trapping party of Ewing Young, whom he left in order to hunt sea otters along the coast. He came to Monterey to have his rifle repaired, met Cooper there and entered into the rental agreement. But after a couple of years Dye found the arrangement unprofitable and left to open a distillery near Santa Cruz.

In August 1851, Cooper found other renters in the persons of Robert H. Fisher, Jose Maria Smith, and Manuel Smith, but Fisher dropped out early, Manuel Smith sold his interest, and only Jose Maria Smith remained, staying into the 1860s.

The agreement signed with the three set forth the conditions whereby the rancho was to be developed:

1. The renters were to assist at all times in taking care of and in corralling all the cattle, horses or other animals belonging to Cooper. They were allowed to use for milking purposes all the cows they could tame, and Cooper would pay them $3 for every wild cow they tamed for milking—over and above the 92 tame cows that were already on the farm.

2. Smith and associates were to be allowed for their consumption and that of their families, three young bulls every two months.

3. They were to build on the place to be chosen by Cooper a good and substantial adobe house, to contain two rooms, each 16

The log house at Andrew Molera State Park, believed to have been built in the 1840s for Captain J.B.R. Cooper.

feet square, with a passageway between, 8 feet in width. The walls were to be 12 feet high from stone foundations. The floor and under part of a loft floor were to be planed, the house well finished with doors and windows and covered with shingles. Smith and company were to supply the labor and materials and Cooper would furnish the iron and glass. When the work was completed Cooper would pay them $600.

4. The renters were to enclose at least 10 acres with a substantial redwood post and rail fence, to be used by them for cultivation and for an orchard which would be planted at Cooper's expense. They would care for, preserve, and have the use of this 10 acres during the rental term, and at the end of the term Cooper would pay them 74 cents for each 8 feet of fencing.

5. Cooper reserved for himself the privilege of occupying, cultivating, and using any part of the farm, not interfering with any part they were using, and Cooper could also kill cattle from stock already on the farm for the consumption of his family.

6. Smith et al would receive from Cooper at the end of the term all the increase over and above 1,150 head. It was noted that there were 600 head of stock on the ranch when they started. The increase would be taken in calves, one half bull, the other half cow calves.

An account book now at Bancroft Library and given by Mrs. John B.R. Cooper, widow of Captain Cooper's grandson, traces the development of the range from 1855 on. The first entry shows eight head of cattle delivered to Pancho Estrada, 126 to John H. Cooper (Captain Cooper's son), 126 to Juan B.R. Cooper, 17 killed for jerky, 18 killed for use on the rancho, some exchanged for a bull, etc. Of the stock that was the personal property of Cooper there was an increase of 106 bull calves and 137 cow calves. Sixteen were sent to his Molino Ranch in Sonoma County, some were ironed (branded) as an increase, and some 41 bull calves and 72 cow calves were listed as tamed. At the same time Jose Maria Smith had added to his herd 53 bull calves and 62 cow calves.

The tools on the rancho were increasing in number. In September 1855, Cooper made a list, which included a whipsaw, cross-cut saw, auger, large iron pots, froe for splitting shingles, plus household items such as 11 plates, cups and saucers, pitcher, tin candlestick, tin coffee pot, tin cup, pint measure, looking glass, iron spits, buckets, etc.

The main problem facing the men operating the ranch, and Cooper himself when overseeing the work, was getting there. Problems of transportation down the long coastal headlands were staggering for cattle, horses, mules, and men. Being used to the sea, Captain Cooper bought a boat and landed his supplies at the mouth of the Big Sur River, where the next generation built a wharf.

His account book shows that in 1855-56 he bought two boats, one of them freighted from San Francisco, for use between Monterey and the ranch. Whether one was a replacement for the other is not known. This was a considerable expense during a

Beach at mouth of Big Sur River. Here freight was hauled ashore from ships delivering goods for Cooper Ranch, and here picnics were held by the Coopers and other pioneer families.

12-month period, totaling about $650, and including a new mast, probably due to coastal storms, and various other repairs. In August 1857, he entered in the Sur account the charge of $40 for a "canoa."

A trail may have been developed along the coast about this time, as an alternate to making landings in a small boat on an often fogbound shore. During the late 1850s the account book also shows cheese being produced at El Sur, the taming of the cows and the resultant dairy herd having paid off. Three cheeses

weighing 20 pounds were kept, and six were delivered to Manuel
Diaz, who had a store adjoining Cooper's home in Monterey.
"Peter the Indian brought from the Sud 160 lbs of cheese," one
entry reads.

One of the inside pages from Cooper's "Labourers Account Book" showing
Cooper's handwriting. (The Bancroft Library, University of California,
Berkeley.)

The list of men employed on the ranch was added to. Christostomo Castro "went to the Sud with his family from Monterey and engaged for one year at $20 per month." Others included David Castro, Sisto Manjares, Narcisso and at least two other Indians named Salvadore and Nickolas. Manuel Boronda went to work "steady" on November 1860 at $20 per month.

The men on the ranch could charge items at the stores in Monterey when they came to town, and those charges were paid by Cooper and deducted from the men's pay when he settled up. For example, when Mateo went to work as "Mateo del Sud" or "Matthew," he evidently took his wife with him as he charged a pair of women's shoes, six yards of cotton, and soap, as well as a rifle, a mould, flour, sugar, a padlock, and some bread. When Andreas came to Monterey he had need of a flannel shirt and a pair of boots, as well as powder and lead.

More land was being brought under cultivation, as the book has entries concerning plows being purchased. One from Honore Escolle cost $14.50. And in February 1859, Cooper paid the storekeeper Joseph Boston $6.72 for barley.

That same year of 1859 marked an important step in the ownership of the ranch. On January 20 a bill was paid "for surveying Sud rancho, $340," and another bill was paid for boat hire for the surveyors. Cooper, along with all other rancho owners, had to present his claim with proof of ownership to the Land Commission appointed by the United States government. The surveying cost was probably to make a complete map of the rancho for presentation to the Commission. According to a report made to the state surveyor-general in 1880, the Rancho El Sur was patented to J.B.R. Cooper May 18, 1866. The final confirmation gave him 8,949.06 acres, always used primarily to raise stock for his other ranches.

Any cattle ranch in an undeveloped country is subject to the raids of predators. The Sur ranch faced the sea, with the tree-covered hills almost enclosing its pasture area. The now extinct

California grizzly bear roamed the hills and was a threat to stock and man.

Cooper paid well for a bear killed. At a time when a mayordomo was receiving $20 a month, Cooper paid to a man named Sandoval in July of 1857, $24 for killing a bear. Sandoval worked on the ranch that year, helping with the matanza (roundup). Another noted killer of bears was Jacobo Escobar. The Escobar brothers were known as being ever ready to capture a bear alive and bring it to Monterey for a bull and bear fight. In July of 1867 Jacobo was on the Sur, and Cooper charged him $90 for two horses, while paying him $70 for killing three bears.

The old account book gives glimpses of the annual cattle drive. Jose Maria Smith was paid $30 for taking charge of cattle to be sold in San Francisco. On his return Cooper settled up with Jose "respecting the provisions he were to have." Aside from the regular hands, others were hired for the drive. Antonio was paid a total of $40 including $1 in cash given him in San Francisco. George Smith earned 75 cents the first day, then $2 per day for 10 days, and another eight days for $12. Jose M. Armenta worked seven days for $1 per day, then four days for $6.

In May 1972, 100 years after Cooper's death, the *Monterey Peninsula Herald* reported that 2,100 acres of the Rancho El Sur had sold for $1,100,000. Five parcels of the Cooper-Molera estate near Castroville, representing about one-eighth of the total there, had sold for $592,000.

Picture shown at left: Guillermo Guadalupe Alfredo Rogers Cooper, known to the family as Rogerio, is pictured with one of his Larkin first cousins (seated). Born February 1, 1838, Rogerio went East for schooling, including a term at Andover. Upon his return to California in 1855 he went to the Sur ranch to learn the family cattle business. The last Monterey area record of him found to date is an entry in the county archives, the death of one Secundino Villa, "pistol shot" by Rogerio Cooper, November, 1860. Rogerio died in Canada, October 6, 1873, having been omitted from his father's will which was probated in 1872. His body was brought back to California for interment with the family. The headstone reads "William R. Cooper, aged 35 years." (Society of California Pioneers.)

Cooper had two sons whom he groomed to take over his property. John B.H. Cooper, the oldest, born in 1830, was the one who helped develop the Salinas lands, and was named in his father's will as one of the executors. The second son was William Rogers Cooper, known to the family as Rogerio. Born in 1838, he was sent east to school, and after two years at Andover, returned to California in May of 1855. In January 1857, when 19, Rogerio was presented with a "pistol six shooter," costing $30, but this is recorded in the "house account." The next reference to him is in the "Sud account" of 1858, which may be the year he was sent to the coast ranch to learn the ways of a cattleman.

In March and April of that year, he suffered a severe but unidentified illness, as Dr. McKee, Dr. Calihan, and Dr. Canfield all presented bills for treating him, and Alexander Taylor, Monterey's druggist, also was listed in the house account. Not until the following year, in July, is Rogerio back at El Sur. A pair of spurs, a new saddle, and a Colt's revolver costing $27.50 were bought for him during the next few months, the revolver being sent to the ranch along with two pounds of tea, one arroba of sugar, some soap, and a bag of flour from his brother John.

There is no further mention of Rogerio in the Sur account book, but in the County Recorder's office in Salinas is an old volume in which the County Coroner listed deaths that required a coroner's investigation. On November 29, 1860, there is an entry showing that Secundino Villa had died, age 25, "pistol shot by Rogerio Cooper." No arrest was made. Was the shooting an accident, or was it self-defense? Or what?

11

MYSTERY AND TRAGEDY

THE Coopers' first child, Ana Maria, a good looking, intelligent girl known familiarly as Anita, became one of the popular young belles of Monterey. She had caught the eye of Midshipman William P. Toler, aide-de-camp to Commodore John Drake Sloat, who raised the United States flag over the Custom House on July 7, 1846, to signal that the western boundary of the United States had been pushed to the Pacific Ocean. It was Toler who climbed the flagpole when the ropes jammed, in order to loose the Stars and Stripes to the breeze.

Officers of the *Savannah*, Sloat's flagship, later gave a ball at the Custom House in celebration of the victory, and there Toler, it is believed, met Anita for the first time. She was nearly 18 years of age. Or, since Toler came out originally with Catesby Jones four years earlier, he may have met her then, though she would have been only 14.

In June of 1847, Ebenezer L. Childs wrote to T.O. Larkin from Boston, saying that a Mr. Toler was to be one of Larkin's neighbors and was coming out to California with his daughters. Childs mentioned that the Midshipman, Toler's son, "had formed an attachment for one of John's daughters."

What happened to this romance is anybody's guess. Probably young Toler was assigned elsewhere by the Navy and never got back to Monterey, but in 1847 James L. Ord arrived in that city, as a surgeon under contract to the Army, specifically Company F of the 3rd Artillery. Ford Ord was named for one of his three brothers, Edward O.C. Ord, later a noted Civil War general.

In addition to his Army duties, Dr. Ord acquired some civilian patients, the Coopers among them, and soon was believed to be both treating and courting Anita. Another of his patients was Manuela Jimeno, a gay and pretty girl slightly younger than Anita. Manuela eloped with another recent addition to Monterey's military garrison, Lt. Alfred Sully, but died tragically on March 28, 1851, as the result, it was thought, of eating a poisoned orange which had been sent to her.

Though Lt. Sully was furious at the time, at Ord, for having told Manuela that he saw no harm in her eating the orange (she had recently become a mother), he and Ord soon became good friends. Even though some Montereyans suspected Ord of some sort of criminal involvement, there was never any proof that he was linked to the gift of the orange.

During the next few years Anita was a frequent visitor at her Larkin cousins' new home in San Francisco. After most of Monterey's males had stampeded to the Gold Rush diggings, that latter city was in the doldrums, and though Thomas Oliver Larkin was one of the delegates to the Constitutional Convention, held at Colton Hall in September and October of 1849, he took little part in the convention sessions and was anxious to move to a metropolis which offered more excitement, activity, and commercial opportunity than Monterey.

The Larkins went out of their way to see that Anita met and was received by San Francisco's families of wealth and culture. In part, this may have been reciprocity for the help and sympathy which the Coopers had shown to the Larkin family when T.O. was captured by rebels under the command of Manuel Castro opposing the change in government, in November 1846, and was held as a hostage until the following January before being released in Los Angeles. Meanwhile his four-year old daughter, Adeline, had died.

A letter he wrote to Cooper in July of 1852 reported that Anita had been to a concert, the theater, and a large ball, and was about to attend another ball and another concert before going to Sonoma. Two years later Anita was visiting the Larkins again and they were trying to persuade her mother, Encarnacion, to

join them. Two months after that, in August 1854, Larkin wrote
to Cooper that Anita was well except for an inflamed eye. "Dr.
Ord can tell what it is. Dr. Ord pays more attention to Anita than
to the others; he takes her and Mrs. Larkin on rides."

So Ord had obviously followed Anita to San Francisco, though
in no hurry to wed, and whether there was an official engagement or not, the families believed that his intentions were
serious.

Imagine the consternation, therefore, when it was learned that
Dr. Ord had married Manuela Jimeno's mother, Dona Angustias
Jimeno, following the death of her husband, Manuel, in 1854, in
Mexico. As the daughter of Don Jose de la Guerra y Noriega of
Santa Barbara, Dona Angustias was a wealthy woman, and Dr.
Ord was said to have "moved in where the money was."

The Ords thenceforth were completely ostracized by the Larkins and the Coopers. Larkin wrote to say his daughter Carolina
was giving a party for some 120 to 130 young people and that no
Ord would be welcome there. (Ord's sister had been among the
original invitees.) Larkin also mentioned "the engagement to
marry in Monterey," which even members of the Ord family had
believed to be a fact, so there were others, outside the Larkin and
Cooper families, who concluded that Anita had been deliberately
jilted.

Her father took her back to San Francisco, and once again her
cousins tried to amuse and entertain her, as balm for her broken
heart.

Anita stayed on with the Larkins, eventually marrying a real
estate broker, Herman Wohler, Sept. 29, 1859. When and where
they first met is unknown, but he had been in San Francisco as
early as August 1851. Two days after their marriage, Cooper
wrote to his friend Pablo de la Guerra in Santa Barbara: "No girl
has suffered more than Anita nor worse treated and her last
novio who lives somewhere near your diggings nearly finished
her in mind and body. God give her happiness and health
through this vale of tears." Ord and his wife had moved to Santa

Herman Wohler, husband of Anita Cooper. German born, he came to California in 1848 and became active in real estate. He served one term in the State
Legislature of 1855 and later had an office in San Francisco from which he
managed his properties, including farm lands in Sonoma County. His home for
some years was on Bush street, San Francisco. He died in that city, June, 1877.
(Society of California Pioneers.)

Barbara, and Anita's father, at least, believed there had been an
official engagement before Ord walked off and wedded the
wealthy widow.

News of Anita's marriage, sent to Cooper relatives in the East,
brought a letter from his step-brother, Ebenezer Childs, who in
earlier years had chided Cooper for almost never writing.

"Very many years ago when you were mate of a ship and I was
a beardless boy," wrote Childs, "you gave me a silk umbrella, the

first I ever owned and I believe the first present of any kind that I ever received." The very warm letter went on to thank Cooper for a gift of wine, "sent from a special vineyard in California," and for money which Cooper had sent to Childs for his help in a land claims case.

By the time of her marriage, Anita was 31, in a day when young women usually married a great deal earlier. Her sister Amelia also waited until she was 31, in 1875, when she married Eusebio Molera. They had two children: Andrew, born August 27, 1875, and Francesca, born October 20, 1879. Neither of these children had any progeny, nor did Anita and Herman Wohler. The only Cooper descendants came from John B. Henry Cooper, the eldest son, who on May 18, 1871, married Martha Brawley. They had four children.

Anita, at the time of her marriage, was apparently managing the 17,892-acre Sonoma ranch, where, on October 18, 1856, her father had given 1,500 acres each to Anita and her sister Amelia, "for love," as the grant stated. Harry A. Lapham, Santa Rosa historian who searched the county records in 1982 for Cooper deeds, stated that he had found about 90 transactions in which John B.R. Cooper transferred property as grantor, beginning as early as 1850. In several cases he sold the land subject to subsequent confirmation of his claim by the United States courts. The ranch was patented April 3, 1858. Between 1850 and 1859 he disposed of about 10,600 acres, Lapham found.

Anita's 1,500 acres contained the mill, and the property "is still known as the Wohler Ranch," Lapham wrote to Amelie Elkinton. "There is a Wohler Bridge that crosses the Russian River near the mill site. When I was young the Wohler Ranch was the largest hop ranch in Sonoma County. Many of the sales Cooper made were to persons who were very prominent in Sonoma County history in later years, as well as some who were well known prior to purchase."

Though several suits against squatters, and against tenants failing in their obligations, were brought in Anita's name, her

Amelia Cooper, daughter of Captain Cooper. Born March 10, 1844, she was baptised as Francisca Guadalupe Amelia. Taught by tutors at home, and music teachers, she also attended the early convent school, St. Catherine's Academy, until it was moved to Benecia. She married Eusebio Molera, April 19, 1875, with her uncle Mariano Vallejo and her elder sister Anita Cooper Wohler as witnesses, the ceremony being performed in Spanish. By 1881, she and her husband lived at 1928 Sacramento St., San Francisco. He in partnership with J.C. Cebrian, had an office on Polk street. Amelia and Eusebio had two children, Andrew and Frances. (Society of California Pioneers.)

Eusebio Molera, husband of Amelia Cooper. Born in Vich, Spain, son of a
general in the Spanish Army, he was graduated from the Academy of Royal
Engineers in 1868. Emigrating to the United States he became prominent in
engineering and architectural circles in San Francisco. He is believed to have
met Amelia when he came to Big Sur to supervise some work on the Point Sur
lighthouse. He was active in the Pacific Union Club, the University Club, a
trustee of the California Academy of Sciences, and received honors in Spain for
his writings on the history of the Spanish in California. He was also a supervisor of the City and County of San Francisco. He died in that city, January 14,
1932. (Society of California Pioneers.)

father's small pocket account books show that he was watching over his two daughters' shares on the Molino Ranch as well as his own. He had been developing orchards there, beginning about 1853, and during that year the first of the squatter suits were filed. His books show that a shipment of bare root trees which he was having sent from the East arrived in Monterey by mistake and then had to be taken up to the El Molino Ranch, much to his annoyance. It cost $19 to ship them from San Francisco to Petaluma, and another $12 from Petaluma to the ranch.

Among the items found in his house after his death was a *Catalogue of Fruits*, published by Honey & Co., horticulturists, of 7 Merchant Row, Boston, dated 1856. The text announced that their nursery was in Cambridge, two miles from the city. As much as 10 years earlier, however, Cooper was having fruit trees shipped, for a letter to him from Faxon Dean Atherton, written at Valparaiso on May 19, 1846, states that Atherton had seen a memorandum of some cherry trees going to Cooper on the bark *Joven Guipuzcoana*. "I suppose it must be old Cooper of Sawmill memory with a bald head and a lame hand, a man who couldn't swear if he tried ever so hard," Atherton wrote.

The Russians at Fort Ross had planted apples, peaches, pears and cherries. By 1840 they had build two hot houses and were raising grapes from cuttings shipped from Lima, and peaches from trees sent from Monterey. Cooper may have followed their example. He was also renting out various parts of El Molino and obtaining a good price from the tenants.

His son John became the workhorse of the family's second generation, overseeing work at El Sur and also at the Bolsa del Potrero ranch in the Salinas-Castroville area. After his marriage in 1871, John built a house in Castroville and made this his headquarters.

His father was one of the first landowners in California to employ Chinese labor, at El Sur and in Sonoma County. After Cooper had sold his Marin County ranches, Nicosia and Corte

Madera, in 1850, Larkin wrote to him from the East the following January:

> I learn that you have sold the Corte Madera Rancho. I am glad of it. Sell another rancho if you can. Senators Benton and Gwin have each a land bill for California before the Senate. It's impossible for us to foretell whether the government will construe titles by the letter or the spirit; if the former, it will prove bad for many landholders. You ought to order Mr. Rogers to invest $20,000 in your wife's name and $20,000 in your own name in real estate here [New York] or in Boston.

Cooper did have money invested in the East, including a store in Boston, but was concentrating on proving his titles in California, in which he was totally successful, over a period of years.

As mentioned in the previous chapter, Rogerio was being trained at El Sur to take a hand in the family's ranch business. But the account book for 1863-64 contains no mention of him, though there are a lot of charges listed for his younger brother Guadalupe. Somewhere during this time Rogerior disappeared from California. Nothing has been found so far to show why, where, or exactly when. The only clue is contained in a letter from Mariano Vallejo in Sonoma to his sister Encarnacion Vallejo Cooper in San Francisco, and dated October 29, 1873.

Vallejo wrote that he had received Encarnacion's letter the previous day, announcing the death of Rogerio in Victoria, B.C. It had caused grief and sadness. They all shed tears. They all loved and sympathized with Rogerio from the heart "not only for being a close relative but also for being so disgraced."

Whatever Rogerio had done was being kept a family secret.

Vallejo went on to say that he hoped his sons, Andronico, Platon, and Uladislao, might be the pallbearers to carry Rogerio's remains, "they loved him from the heart." He offered whatever help he could, saying that he knew what it was to lose three sons. Francisca (Francisca Carrillo, Vallejo's wife) and Salvador (his and Encarnacion's brother) joined Encarnacion in her sorrow, he added, inviting Encarnacion, Anita, and Amelia to visit the

Vallejos at Lachryma Montis (his home in Sonoma) after the funeral."We would try to alleviate their grief."

(The letter is from "A Calendar of Family Correspondence," a thesis written in 1975 by Edith Ann Evans.)

This is the great mystery in the Cooper family history. Was Rogerio banished for some crime or unforgivable deed that he had committed? Did his father cut him off without the proverbial penny? Cooper's will, dated June 14, 1871, stated that he intentionally omitted to provide for his son, William Rogers Cooper (Rogerio), "relying upon his mother to make such provisions as she thinks necessary."

The pistol shooting of Secundino Villa by Rogerio in November 1860 could scarcely have been the cause of banishment, for no action was taken at the time and Rogerio was at home for at least two years after that. But why did his father hire a detective nearly 10 years later? An entry in the account book for May 19, 1870, reads "Pd. detective for looking after Harry [?], $29.30." Who was Harry? (The name may have been Harvey. Cooper's handwriting is difficult to decipher.)

All that is known is that Rogerio died in Victoria, British Columbia, October 6, 1873. The cause of his death was listed as pneumonia. The following year, the body was brought to the family plot in Colma, California, and re-interred. Date of death is shown on the headstone.

The only reference to Victoria, B.C. in the account books is an entry at the back of one of them, dated circa 1865: "Care Millie and Fogel, New England Bakery, Victoria." This, it appears, was where Rogerio could be reached. As to who Millie and Fogel were, no one at this point knows.

Equally mysterious and tragic was the fate of Guadalupe.

The "house account" for 1862 show that on March 26, "Guadalupe commenced school," his father paying $2 to Schoolmaster McCloud for one month's schooling. Guadalupe, just 13, may have been educated at home previously.

Cooper had been one of several Monterey parents trying to

have a dependable school established for their children. His house account book which opens with a date of August 14, 1855, shows $100 paid to Mr. Hanson, schoolmaster, for Amelia, Guadalupe, and Alfred (Larkin) on October 20. At the same time Juan Hartnell was paid $32. Hanson received $88 the following July 3, and Hartnell $60. In 1857 Guadalupe "went to school to the Judge Merritt," who in November of that year "commenced to teach in house" and was paid both in cash and with "four trees." Later entries show a music teacher paid $20 and another $3 "for tuning piano." In 1860 Judge Rumsey becomes Guadalupe's teacher and in 1862 a "Mr. Loud," followed by Ambrosio Gomez in 1863. On August 27 of that year, Cooper paid $1.50 "for photograph of schoolhouse and children."

Some time in 1864 the Coopers moved from Monterey to a house which he had had built at 821 Bush St., San Francisco. His half-brother, Larkin, had died of a fever in San Francisco, at his home on Stockton Street, October 17, 1858, at the age of 56. Now, six years later, Cooper had decided, like Larkin before him, that the future lay in San Francisco rather than in Monterey.

The account book shows expenditures from 1867 through 1869 for Guadalupe, for clothes, boots, harness, a fishing pole, etc., and simply "cash." In June 1869, his father took him East. A letter from Cooper to his daughter Anita written on June 16 reports that he "arrived at Boston with Guadalupe this a.m. Saw troops receiving [President Ulysses S.] Grant and parade. If you write, do so c/o J.P. Leese."

At this time Guadalupe had had two years of college (which college is not certain), and the trip may have been a reward for good grades.

Less than three months later, on September 9, the *Monterey Gazette* broke the news of his death, under a special heading, "In Memoriam:"

Our community was horror stricken Thursday morning (8) by the receipt of a dispatch announcing the death of Guadalupe J. Cooper-a young gentleman born and raised in this city. From the San Francisco papers of the 9th we glean the

following scant particulars of his demise. It seems that he was making prepara-
tions to leave for this city and repaired to the barn to clean his revolver.
Sometime afterwards a servant discovered his lifeless body lying on the floor,
with his revolver—of which one barrel was empty—beside him. It is supposed
that while he was engaged in loading it one chamber of the pistol was acciden-
tally discharged—the ball entering his mouth and penetrating the brain and
this is all that is known of the last end of one to whose view nothing but the
bright side of life had as yet been presented. Just entering upon his twentieth
year and the idol of his parents and relatives and the favorite of Fortune's
brightest smiles, in one moment Guadalupe passed from time to eternity ... Of
an impulsive but generous disposition he had many friends and few enemies.

The *Alta Californian*, in San Francisco, carried a brief obituary
and announced that the funeral "will take place from St. Mary's
Cathedral, at 10 o'clock this morning (Friday the 9th). Friends
and acquaintances are respectfully invited to attend without
further notice."

Whether the explanation of the cause of death was entirely
plausible, it was accepted by those close to the family, such as
David Spence, who wrote an immediate letter of condolence to
Cooper and his wife, from Monterey.

In the correspondence and other records of the Cooper family,
the name of Herman Wohler, Anita's husband, appears infre-
quently and finally disappears altogether. A year after their
marriage he was writing from San Francisco to Amelia, Anita's
sister, in Monterey, passing on information such as "Saw Cooper
on Russian River. He wants Amelia, John and Encarnacion to go
to San Francisco at once."

The only other scanty information brought to light about
Wohler was the fact that he was nominated for and took part in
the Democratic Legislative Convention in 1855 and served in the
third and seventh sessions of the California State Assembly. He
died June 2, 1877.

12

HISTORY OF THE COOPER ADOBE
AND ITS FURNISHINGS

THOUGH the Coopers moved to San Francisco in 1864, they retained their Monterey home, first with William Hamel as caretaker, then later George Austin. Hamel had come to Monterey about 1846-47 with Company F of the 3rd U.S. Artillery. Austin, who succeeded him, had been a midshipman on the *Independence* in 1847 and originally came from Boston.

A Monterey town house came in handy for Cooper and Larkin, both of whom were constantly on the move. As early as June 16, 1857, Larkin wrote to Cooper, "I was a week in Monterey. Slept in your home. As the living and the attendance in the hotel is bad, the two lawyers [who accompanied Larkin] found your house a godsend. The man keeps both house and yard in very good order." So even before the Coopers made San Francisco their base, they were leaving Hamel in charge when they were away from Monterey.

The history of the house, which now is a basic part of the Cooper-Molera Adobe, is still being unraveled, as the State Department of Parks and Recreation completes the renovation of the entire complex at Munras Avenue and Polk Street.

In July of 1828, two letters crossed each other. One, written July 21 by Seth Rogers from San Diego to Cooper in Monterey included the sentence, "I want to know how you come with your house and other concerns." The next day in Monterey, Cooper was writing in part as follows to William G. Dana of Rancho Nipomo, in San Luis Obispo County.

"I hope we shall meet shortly. I shall have a place to put you in about 6 months, big enough for both."

The exact site of this 1828 house has not been established, but foundations found under the present adobe, and of an earlier date than the adobe, may indicate the location.

Among the documents found in the Cooper house were several account books, including a "Labourers Account" which shows that at least 36 men were working for Cooper in 1831-32, including Indians who made adobe bricks, carpenters, lumbermen delivering sawed boards, etc. Most of these accounts were closed out during the spring of 1832, indicating a large project concluded.

October 22, 1833, Cooper signed a deed conveying half of the house to John Coffin Jones. The deed sets forth in part that Cooper, "being the owner of the house he occupies in this place, built at his own expense in the year 1832, on a lot granted by the Ayuntamiento ... he does give in solemn sale unto the said Jones the one half of the aforesaid house which lies towards the northwest containing five rooms, and one half of the corral."

The part of the house sold—Jones was already occupying it—was 40 feet fronting on Munras by 48 in depth. The corral part sold was 142 feet deep by 37 feet in width. Jones was obligated to build a kitchen and also to dig a well in order to retain possession. It was specified that the house had a tile roof.

This sold portion passed through several hands. Jones sold it to Nathan Spear in 1836. From Spear it passed to Manuel Diaz in 1845; from Diaz to David Spence in 1855. Finally it was purchased back into the Cooper family by Anita Cooper Wohler in June 1900, and was passed by her to her niece, Frances Molera, to join the whole together again.

The other half of the house built by Cooper in 1832 was changed to a full two-story house in the early 1850s. Cooper bought from the Diaz family one half of the entryway between the two halves, a piece of land five feet wide, in order to have room to put his stairway up to the second floor. This necessitated

Frances Mary Molera, daughter of Eusebio and Amelia, was born October 20, 1879. She was interested in California history and was active in the Women's Auxiliary of the Society of California Pioneers, also was a member of the California Historical Society and of the Alumnae of the Convent of the Sacred Heart in San Francisco. She made it possible for some 2,000 acres of the El Sur Rancho to be saved through the Nature Conservancy and her gifts. The park established is named for her brother, Andrew Molera. She left the original Cooper family home in Monterey to the National Trust for Historic Preservation, having kept the property intact for many years. She died October 1, 1968, and is buried in the family plot at Holy Cross Cemetery, Colma. (Society of California Pioneers.)

closing up a door into the Diaz house. This door was just covered over and was found during restoration, complete with hardware, framing, etc.

In order to enlarge his corral area, Cooper purchased from a neighbor, Gabriel de le Torre, a strip of land from Polk Street to the canyon known as Hartnell Gulch. This was in January 1842. Yet another strip of additional land was added to the town house property by Cooper on September 16, 1863, when he bought a strip of land, which included the canyon, from Rafael Estrada. This land is still part of the property but lies outside the adobe walls and today is leased by Safeway as part of its parking lot.

There are several questions that arise. When was the so-called Spear warehouse built along Polk? According to a letter written by Miss Molera, this was the first structure her grandfather put up, in 1826, on the property. This building is not listed in the deed from Cooper to Jones. But it shows in the 1842 lithograph which Larkin had made, locating the buildings of Monterey, and it is listed there as Spear property.

During the years the Diaz family had the former Spears part of the property, stores were added at the corner of Polk and Munras. The rents of these helped support Mrs. Diaz during her lifetime.

The census of 1860 gave Monterey's total population as 1,653, though stating that more than 10 per cent of the houses were unoccupied. Occupants of the Cooper establishment were listed as John B.R. Cooper, age 67, retired shipmaster, real estate valued at $65,560, personal estate $44,750; his wife, Incarnacion V., age 49; Anita C. Wholer, 30 (spellings were frequently incorrect); Juan Cooper, 29; Rogerio Cooper, 22; Amelia Cooper, 15; Guadalupe Cooper, 11; Ana McMahon, 7; Antonio Cornellio, 49, servant; Herman Wholer, real estate agent, born in Mecklenburgh.

The little McMahon girl had been taken into the Cooper household after her father, Jeremiah, had been killed in Monterey's most celebrated shootout. His opponent was Dr. Henry L. Sanford, who had accused McMahon's brother-in-law, William

The two-story Cooper house, Monterey, some time prior to 1900, with the story-and-a-half Diaz adobe to its right, and the two-story Alvarado adobe at the far right. (Slevin collection, Bancroft Library, University of California, Berkeley.)

Roach, former Monterey County sheriff, of absconding with $84,654 in gold dust, entrusted to him as guardian of Sanford's wife's estate. In a confrontation at the Washington Hotel, McMahon and Sanford fired simultaneously and both fell, each with a bullet through the heart. In a long and involved feud over the missing gold dust, 15 men were killed, including one who was hanged from an oak tree behind J.B.R. Cooper's house. The gold dust was never found.

McMahon's widow died in December 1859, leaving her daughter, Ana, an orphan.

There were others who enjoyed the Cooper hospitality through the years. On January 25, 1854, Maria Antonia Lugo de Vallejo, Encarnacion's mother, signed her will at her residence,

Fan window in north end of Cooper attic. (Marcia DeVoe photo.)

"the house of J.B.R. Cooper in Monterey." She died May 7, 1855, regretting that she could not look upon Rogerio before her passing. Rogerio, her favorite, arrived 11 days later from the East.

Through much of the Cooper story, his wife, Encarnacion, moves like a wraith-like figure in the background. It is difficult to reconstruct her personality, and the two portraits of her extant,

Detail of fan-shaped window. (Marcia DeVoe photo.)

one an oil painting, part of a matching pair with her husband, show her in her old age. She was an ardent Roman Catholic, as befitted her family background, worried that her children might stray from the true faith, particularly Rogerio who went East to school.

Whether she ever became fluent in English is doubtful. Her husband spoke and wrote to her in Spanish, and she felt most at home among friends with a Spanish and Mexican background. This was particularly true after the Coopers moved to San Francisco, where, the Larkins had assured her, she would find many Spanish-speaking neighbors. She contributed freely and regularly to the church, as the account books show, and was always among the first to be called on for support.

On December 16, 1857, Cooper's old friend and associate James Hunnewell had written to some friends, the Ruggleses, "The great rise in value of land and cattle in California has made

Front door of Cooper house, 1974

Mr. Cooper a very wealthy man." Hunnewell, who had returned
to Charlestown, Mass. from Honolulu, and had himself become a
man of wealth and standing, should have known, but whether
Cooper would have agreed with him is questionable.

When Nathan Spear bought John C. Jones' half of the Cooper
house, November 14, 1836, he paid $2,000 "in cowhides." This

Top: Rear of Diaz Adobe, after removal of old roof, 1981. (Marcia DeVoe photo.)

Bottom: Reconstruction work in progress on Cooper-Molera-Diaz adobes, 1982. (Marcia DeVoe photo.)

Top: Reconstruction work on the Cooper-Molera adobe, as seen from Simoneau Plaza, 1982. (Marcia DeVoe photo.)

Bottom: Sign on Polk street near Alvarado, explaining restoration work on Cooper-Molera Adobe.

was typical of the kind of "non-cash" deals that were made, and the reason Cooper sold to Jones in the first place was that he owed him $3,136, as a promissory note showed. He may have been thus arranging to pay for the cargo of Jones' ship, the *Volunteer*. But he did not feel for many years that he was in any respect "a wealthy man," if ever.

As late as 1862 he was keeping careful track of the fact that he had to pay a federal "pole" tax for his son John and himself of $2 each, which went up to $3 each in 1864, and in 1865 jumped to $4 just for John, for "military and pole tax." On December 4, 1863, he paid an income tax of $90.20.

Accustomed to cramped quarters aboard ship, with little furniture or other conveniences, Cooper is believed to have started married life with a minimum of furnishings in his and Encarnacion's home.

In 1835 Richard Henry Dana came along the California coast in a hide-and-tallow trader, and afterward reported thusly:

> The floors are generally of earth, the windows grated and without glass; and the doors, which are seldom shut, open directly into the common room, there being no entries. Some of the more wealthy inhabitants have glass in the windows and board floors; and in Monterey nearly all of the houses are whitewashed on the outside. The better houses, too, have red tiles upon the roofs. The common ones have two or three rooms which open into each other, and are furnished with a bed or two, a few chairs and tables, a looking glass, a crucifix, and small daubs of paintings enclosed in glass representing some miracle of martyrdom. They have no chimneys or fireplaces in the houses, and all their cooking is done in a small kitchen, separated from the house.

When Mariano Vallejo was helping Henry Cerruti obtain material for Bancroft's *History of California*, they visited the widow of Luis Antonio Arguello, who had married in 1819. As to furniture, she claimed that the poor people did not feel the want of it, because they did not know its use. She added that the Arguello, Amesti, Alvarado, de la Guerra, and several other families of note had possessed since 1824 large bureaus, large looking glasses, and tables inlaid with shells, which sailing vessels brought from China and from Peru. Chinese dishes and bowls were in use in homes that could afford them.

On the same trip, Vallejo and Cerruti visited Vallejo's sister, Mrs. Jacob P. Leese, in Monterey. "In her salon," Cerruti wrote, "I noticed many bureau lamps, tables, pictures and boxes of Chinese make ... She said that French or American furniture was not to be had in the country, and therefore she had no choice but to furnish her apartments with articles of Chinese make."

There was hardly a home of any means that did not contain at least one of the brightly painted leather-covered camphorwood chests or trunks that came in nests from China. The lack of closets made it necessary to have chests in which to store clothing, linens, etc. It was about this same period that a few of the Chinese lacquered sewing boxes and tables began to appear. The finely carved ivory needle cases, bobbins, and bead and sequin boxes in these sewing sets are often of exquisite workmanship.

It is difficult to tell from Cooper's account books which of these items he brought from Canton for resale, and which for Encarnacion. In the Pacific House there is a marble-topped table which he brought for Joseph Boston, similar to one which he also obtained for his own house. There is also a Chinese sewing cabinet with dragon feet in Pacific House, and a similar one in the Stevenson House, with a bag hung under the table to hold yarn and other materials.

As trading ships and whaling ships increased in numbers, and the owners realized the demands of California, more furniture was brought here to trade for hides and tallow, and for feed and other supplies. Some families of means had fine pieces by the 1840s, but the quantity was limited.

Sir George Simpson, visiting Monterey in 1842, wrote:

Externally the habitations have a cheerless aspect in consequence of the paucity of windows, which are almost unattainable luxuries. Glass is rendered dear by the exorbitant duties ...

Among the California housewives the bed is quite a show, enjoying as it does, the full benefit of contrast. While other furniture consists of a deal table and some badly made chairs, with probably a Dutch clock and an old looking glass, the bed ostentatiously challenges admiration with its snowy sheets fringed with lace, its piles of soft pillows covered with finest linens or the richest satin, and

its well arranged drapery and tasteful curtains. its wool mattress is the strong-
hold of millions of fleas.

Visiting Governor Alvarado, Sir George reported: "We were
ushered into his excellency's apartment, which contained a host
of common chairs, a paltry table, a kind of sofa, large Dutch clock,
and four or five cheap mirrors."

Jack Swan, who arrived in Monterey in 1843 and was to build
the adobe now known as the First Theatre, described the town as
he first saw it: "But few of the houses had windows with glass,
and still fewer chimneys; glass panes in windows being the
exception, and iron or wooden bars in the windows being the
rule, according as the owners were rich or poor."

In April of 1844, Thomas O. Larkin sent east a list of furniture
that he wished to obtain for his two-story adobe. Here is the list
of what may have been the furnishings of the first home "in the
American style" in California:

> 4 doz chairs, with arm and rocking chairs
> 1 pair of sofas, 6½ or 7 feet long
> 1 pair of sofas that can be used as beds
> 2 ladies' work tables
> 2 wash hand stands
> 1 pair large dining tables for a hall
> 1 pair heavy round tables
> 2 pairs mirrors, each different pattern
> 4 large National pictures, handsome frames
> 4 pair large candlesticks of different patterns,
>   large glass shades.

When John C. Jones bought half of the Cooper house, he added
a window, which cost him $12 for the glass and $4 for cutting and
setting it. He also papered one room, the paper costing $8.50 and
labor $13. Furthermore, he paid $20 for building a chimney,
though it is not clear whether this was for the house or the
separate cookhouse.

British transfer print, "Tiger Hunt," 1840-1860.

Maker's mark on reverse of platter, "Tiger Hunt."

Ceramic finds by archaeologists during reconstruction of Cooper-Molera adobe. (Photos by Marcia DeVoe.)

Chinese export, "Canton Porcelain."

"Old Blue" ceramics, circa 1830, and blue bottle.

Children's toy pitcher and cup.

Chinese export porcelain, circa 1830.

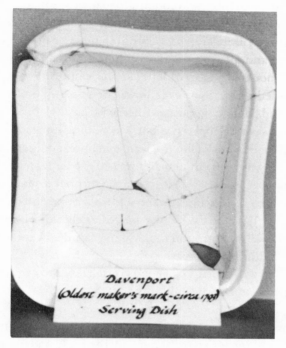

Serving dish, Davenport, oldest maker's mark found at site, circa 1773.

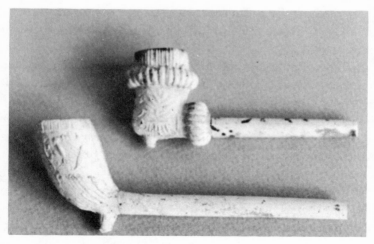

Two of several pipes found.

, and cooking, usually took place in a small, _ng, sometimes with a horno (bake oven in _gside, and a broiling pit. The pit was dug into _eat suspended on long spits across the pit and _als. Iron cooking stoves came later. Vegetables were _ using two large bowls or pans, one of them for cleaning a._ peeling, the other filled with clear water into which vegetables were put until the pot was boiling or ready.

The metate with mano was an ever-present item in early kitchens. It was kept on a low, home-made table, with a short-legged chair or stool beside it. Here the mother or daughters sat to grind the corn. The stone mano was used as we do a rolling pin. A platter or large flat dish was placed at the lower end of the metate to catch the ground corn. Many families kept in use for years the old Indian mortars, particularly those who had Indian servants. It was the mark of a good housekeeper to grind the corn at least twice, to remove all lumps.

A large part of the cooking was done on "hornillas," or little ovens, consisting of two layers of stone held together by mud, laid about 12 to 14 inches apart, about 8 inches high, and perhaps two feet long. A large iron plate called a "comal" was used to stretch across the hornilla and served the same purpose as the top of a stove. On this plate were cooked the beans and pesole (corn and beans mixed).

Garlic was pulled from the ground, the dirt shaken off, and three plants plaited and tied together, then three again, etc., until there was a long string of garlic to hang from the rafters of the kitchen. Other plants for seasoning were also hung in bunches or bags. Thus the housewife had them all within easy reach. Floors of kitchens were dirt for many years. Wooden planks were put down in the 1870-80 period.

Water was hauled in a large barrel with a horse and wooden sled. The barrel was set outside the kitchen door and kept covered. Beside it was a pot or bucket to dip the water out. Country homes usually had a well, but if possible drinking water was hauled from a clear nearby stream. In town, as the houses began to crowd each other and the wells went dry or became contaminated, the town folk used a town well.

For washing clothes, there were two soap roots, amole and jamatal. The amole was pear-shaped and small. The jamatal was as large as a man's head. Both of these were very strong and astringent and used only for a first soaping. Then good rinsing had to be done and common soap used again, or the clothes would leave a rash on the body, like poison oak. The washing was done on a board 18 or 20 inches wide and about three feet long, perfectly smooth, placed alongside a running stream.

Near the northeastern outskirts of Monterey was Washer-woman's Bay, to which the ladies took their clothes to be washed. There they spent the day pounding and rubbing, rinsing, rewashing with home-made soap and drying by spreading the garments out on bushes in the sun. This was also a favorite place for news and gossip to be exchanged, while eating a picnic lunch.

Though bathrooms as known today were non-existent, Californians did bathe, in a nearby stream if they lived on a ranch, or in a small wooden shelter built next to a well if they lived in town. This shelter was closed on three sides and open on the fourth, with wooden benches on which the bather sat naked while water was dipped out of a barrel and poured over the head. After vigorous scrubbing with soap, there came a rinsing with fresh water and the bather was ready for another week. In the winter, a sponge bath was possible from a tub of water in the kitchen. The toilet was an outdoor privy.

By the 1840s, a few families had wash stands, with bowl and pitcher. On ranches there was usually a wooden bench which held a bowl, a bucket of water, and a bit of soap, and which stood on the porch near the back door so that one could wash before meals.

The adobe floors (before the time of wooden floors) were sprinkled daily with water and swept with brooms made from bushes tied tightly together. Adobe houses were built with open ceilings; that is, the rafters were exposed, and the boards above them were the floor boards of the room above, or of an attic area. Thus there was the problem of dust sifting down from above. To control this, the Californians stretched material below the rafters and to nailing strips around the walls. Both yerga (lightweight canvas) and manta (unbleached cotton) were used. Here the dust of years accumulated.

Though candles were the common lighting arrangement for the early houses, whale-oil lamps and pressed-lard lamps came into use after the whaling ships became frequent visitors along the coast. Kerosene was not available until after 1859, and then it cost $1 per gallon, in the East.

If a Monterey family was going to entertain—and everyone did—it might be necessary to borrow all the neighborhood chairs possible. One of the guests at a dance at the Larkin house in the 1840s reported that there were so many people that Mrs. Larkin had large pumpkins brought in and put along the walls for seats between dances.

With the addition to the Cooper adobe of a second full floor in 1850, he splurged a little on additional furnishings. Having sold his Nicasio and Punta de Quentin ranchos, he had some spare cash for a change, and bought a piano and a guitar, among other extravagances. He carpeted the house—not common in adobes—and while in San Francisco in May and June of 1855, he purchased a bureau, a bed, and a pillow. In December of that year, while on a trip to San Jose, he bought an additional seven yards of carpet.

In October he paid $40 for "a stove for cooking," and in January 1856, he bought a bedstead, a mattress, pillows, two chairs, "one bathing tub"—not a usual frill—some bread baskets, and "two sticks for newspapers."

He subscribed to *The Home Journal*, the *Santa Cruz Sentinel*, the *Monterey Democrat*, the *San Jose Mercury,* and *Monterey Union* during the period 1859-64, as well as ordering magazines sent from New York.

Every early California family had at least one carreta, which

Molera family coach, Monterey. (Society of California Pioneers.)

was the only wheeled vehicle in California for many years. The yoke for the oxen was shaped from one piece of wood, and fastened by thongs or rope to the head and horns of the animals.

In July, 1857, Cooper paid for repairs on a buggy and bought a carriage for $255. In July 1859, he bought another buggy for $130 while in San Francisco. A dozen chairs cost him $24. by April of 1860 he was having his stable floored and racks built on it. In March 1863, he paid $6 for a pigeon house. Unfortunately, from time to time in later years his granddaughter, Frances Molera, grew tired of the clutter of papers, memos, clipboards, stacked with notes and other memorabilia, and threw them out or burned them. As a result, there are few records remaining of what he bought for his other houses and workers' buildings at El Molino, Moro Cojo, and El Sur.

In the records that do exist, there is mention of furniture repairing. Nothing, it appeared, was ever discarded or replaced.

Frank Lang with brougham found in Cooper-Molera barn in 1970

"Making do" was inherent in Cooper's New England upbringing, and Encarnacion had gone through many lean years that reinforced in her the California attitude of simplicity about the house.

As for a garden, there were a few decorative fruit trees in the Monterey back yard, and the account books have some references to "fixing up the yard" or "cleaning up the yard." At all the Cooper properties. planting was primarily for food purposes—fruits, vegetables, grain—rather than for decoration.

In later years, grandson Andrew Molera was blamed for many of the broken chairs. At 6 feet 2 inches tall and weighing more than 400 pounds, a center on the University of California varsity

Andrew Molera, son of Eusebio and Amelia, was born August 27, 1877. He attended the University of California at Berkeley, in the class of 1899, and was center on the varsity football team. He introduced the raising of artichokes on the family lands in the Castroville area. He was a well-known host in San Francisco and on his ranches in Monterey County, and was a member of the original Old Chapter Club of Monterey. He died in San Francisco, October 8, 1931, his sister and his father surviving him. (Society of California Pioneers.)

football team, he had only to sit on a chair to destroy it. Alfred E. Priddy, who was Molera's foreman and man-of-all-work at El Sur, said that "no one wanted him around because he broke all the chairs." Andrew loved parties, both at the Monterey adobe and at the Sur ranch, "but the place would be a wreck afterwards," Priddy recalled. Finally, when the adobe became too dilapidated to suit him, and because it had no heating system, Andrew left it to his sister to care for, and moved to Salinas.

He was credited with starting the artichoke business in Castroville, with artichoke plants brought in from Fort Bragg, and Italian farmers to work them.

13

THE LATER YEARS—THE FAMILY TREE

DESPITE the fact that the Gold Rush of '49 drew increasing numbers of Monterey males to the Sierra, and that T.O. Larkin decided that San Francisco held more promise than Monterey, there was still a great deal of activity in the old capital during the early 1850s. Mining for many of the men, was a seasonal occupation, and when the snows and rains became too frustrating up in the hills, they headed back to town for a few months.

There were enough of them on hand to throw a farewell party for Brig. Gen. Bennett Riley in July 1850, and to present him wih a medal and a chain of gold nuggets in recognition of his acumen and statesmanship in heading the Constitutional Convention of 1849. As ex-officio civil governor, Riley had seen the urgent necessity for forming a California government on a broader base than what existed after Commodore Sloat's takeover of the territory in the name of the United States, with only hazy directives from Washington.

In December 1849, following ratification of the constitution by the people of California, Riley declared the new government established and relinquished his office to Peter H. Burnett, who had been elected as the first civil governor of the State. California, Riley said, could not wait indefinitely for a dilatory Congress to approve the move, but he remained in Monterey until July to see that everything was operating satisfactorily.

Juan B.R. Cooper was among those paying tribute to Riley at a civic banquet in the Pacific Building and also took part in the Fourth of July celebration, the first after the adoption of the State Constitution.

On June 6, 1850, a petition from prominent citizens of Monterey was presented to the Council. A copy, now in the historical archives of the Huntington Library in San Marino, reads as follows:

> Whereas, the approaching anniversary of American independence is near at hand,
>
> Whereas, in our Opinion it is a day that should be held sacred by every American—on which should be held up to the minds of the rising generation, the heroes of the Revolution and the authors of our federal constitution and the union it established, as Patriots whom they ought to reverence. The works themselves as political institutions which deserve their veneration, and as Object of commemoration.
>
> We therefore pray, that your honorable body will make an appropriation for the purpose of defraying in part, the expenses necessarily to be incurred in making suitable arrangements for celebrating the 75th Anniversary of American Independence, at this City on the 4th of July next. City of Monterey June 6th, 1850.

This was the year that Lt. Sully designed the arms of the City of Monterey, which he painted to be used in the Fourth of July procession. This procession assembled in the plaza in front of the church, with the band of the 2nd Infantry at its head, preceded by the banner carried by one Dennis McCarty. There was also a mounted escort of young men wearing red "bandas" or "fajas" across the breast. The march proceded to the home of General Riley, who received it in full uniform girded with the yellow sash won at Chapultepec, as a battlefield hero of the Mexican War. He was received with drums rolling and banners waving, and took his place in the line which wended its way to Colton Hall. Ceremonies there consisted of a reading of the Declaration of Independence by Captain E.K. Kane of the Army, followed by a translation into Spanish by Lt. Hamilton; an oration by John A. McDowell, and some remarks in Spanish by the Rev. Padre Ramirez, in his Dominican habit, plus some national airs by the band.

"It was an unusually fine day and we were in fine spirits and our hopes ran high," a former Monterey resident described the event for the *Alta Californian* twenty years later.

Also in 1850 the first federal census was held in Monterey and the first assessor's roll was drawn up.

After California became the nation's 31st state, on September 9, 1850, one of the first duties of the newly elected legislature was to divide the state into counties. A special committee headed by General Mariano G. Vallejo had recommended the boundaries of an original 18 counties: San Diego, Los Angeles, Santa Barbara, San Luis Obispo, Monterey, San Francisco, San Jose, Mount Diablo, Sonoma, Benicia, Sacramento, Sutter, Butte, Fremont, San Joaquin, Redding, Oro, and Mariposa. Name changes, additions, and divisions eventually expanded the number of counties to 58.

The Rev. Samuel Hopkins Willey, who was an alternate chaplain at the Constitutional Convention, established a Sunday School and conducted the first Presbyterian services at Colton Hall, built by another chaplain, Walter Colton, U.S.N., Congregational minister, historian, author and editor, and Monterey's first alcalde to be elected under the United States flag.

Amelia Cooper attended the first convent school in Monterey, St. Catherine's Academy, established in 1851 by three Dominican nuns, but it moved away in 1854. A religious book inscribed to her by the Sisters was found in the Cooper-Molera adobe.

The first public school in Monterey was established in 1854-55 in El Cuartel, a two-story building on Munras Avenue across from the Cooper residence. El Cuartel had served previously as the Mexican military barracks and later as U.S. Army headquarters.

All of these signs of progress should have pointed to the bright future foreseen for Monterey on July 4, 1850, but by the mid 1850s the city was in a slump again. It was no longer the capital. At the 1849 convention various suggestions had been made for a permanent legislative center for the new state, among them San Jose, San Luis Obispo, and Benecia, the last of these founded by Mariano Vallejo, who had named it for his wife, Francisca Benecia Carillo. San Jose won by a vote of 23 to 14, but had no building

Presented to Miss
Amelia Cooper
for her good conduct
by the Sisters of St
Catharine's Academy
Monterey Jul. 25. 1852

Cover and inside page of school book used by Cooper children.

.ept a partly furnished hotel that was
After a very rainy winter, it was voted to
the new town of Vallejo, which also had no
It was then agreed that the new legislature
ᴊacramento.

ʟ   .ıento was flooded, so in May 1853, Benecia was
declareᴄ ⸝ be the seat of government. Sacramento, however,
which had become an important incorporated city and center of
trade and transportaion, made a new bid and won.

Whether Cooper was involved in any of this political shuffling
and re-shuffling is doubtful. He was constantly on the move. On
October 30, 1852, he was shipping three California grizzly bears
to South America via the *Venice*. The invoice, found in the
Cooper-Molera adobe, shows that "one large mountain California grizzly, one cinnamon, female, and one young tame bear,"
captured by James Adams (later known as "Grizzly Adams")
were freighted from Sonora to Stockton and then shipped to
Lima, Peru, in iron-bound cages, at a total cost of $6,440. Cooper
knew someone who was willing to pay that large sum , probably
for a zoo or circus. Some time in 1855 he purchased the 13,000-
acre San Bernabe Ranch near King City and turned it over to his
son John to operate. Late in 1855 he was up on the Russian River,
admiring the fruit trees at El Molino. On July 29, 1856, he wrote
to Larkin, "I have been at the Sud Rancho for some time and am
going again."

Cooper had heard from Larkin in March of that year that "your
Northern Rancho [Russian River] was confirmed yesterday for
10½ leagues by Judge Hoffman...I send by mail the *Chronicle*
with the names of the eleven ranches confirmed that day...The
house on your Washington Street land [San Francisco] is nearly
up. It looks pretty well in front and well inside as far as I can see.
With love to the family..."

The news about confirmation of his Sonoma ranch ownership
by the U.S. Land Claims court must have been welcome to
Cooper, who had gone to great pains to have his boundaries

established before the Land Commission. Bolsa del Potrero was confirmed in 1859 and El Sur in 1866.

A letter from David Spence in Monterey to Larkin in San Francisco dated June 14, 1856, says "I suppose you are startled at so many murders, lynchings, etc., in and about our once quiet Monterey, the same as we are at your sad excitement in San Francisco. Where will it all end?"

The next month, Cooper, writing to Larkin, asks him when the Vigilante Committee in San Francisco is going to disband. There had been some talk, during the Roach-McMahon-Sanford feud, of founding a similar committee in Monterey. Larkin replied that "we expect the V. Committee will break up their outward show next week and retire to their homes, but continue their organization for some months. Eben writes it is a bad example but thinks had he been there that under the circumstances he should have been with them."

As early as June 1853, Lt. Alfred Sully, returning to Monterey after a tour of duty at Benicia, had decided that the old Monterey, a peaceful harbor surrounded by tree-topped hills and the scent of pine and salt air, would never be the same again. "The place was filled with Chinamen, catching fish and abalone," he wrote. "These they ship to San Francisco to be consumed by their countrymen. I suppose at and near Monterey there must be at least 300 of them. It looks like a second Canton and smells like a fish market."

Fifteen Chinese coolies had been brought to California by Jacob P. Leese, who accompanied Cooper on his final voyage of the *Eveline*, in 1849-50. They came from Canton on the brig *Mary* and were accompanied by some Chinese house servants.

The year Cooper finally moved to San Francisco, 1864, was the year of the big drought, which, according to his friend William G. Dana of Rancho Nipomo, wiped out some of California's cattle barons. Whether this had anything to do with Cooper's move is a matter for speculation. Also, it was at about this time that Rogerio's name disappeared from the account books. Had his

John B. Rogers Cooper in a rare photograph taken during his later years. Note the formal attire and dark glasses. (Society of California Pioneers.)

crime—whatever it was—made it advisable for the family to leave Monterey? It does not seem to have affected his elder brother, John B.H. Cooper, who served for several years as a Monterey County supervisor, though John eventually moved from Castroville to San Francisco, to a home at the corner of Sacramento and Gough, just one block from the home of his

mother, Encarnacion Vallejo de Cooper. He retained the Castroville residence, however.

Juan Bautista Rogers Cooper's latter years were uneventful.
The captain had left the sea, its hazards and adventures. Apart
from the tragedy of Guadalupe's death and the mystery surround-
ing Rogerio, Cooper's concerns were those of a typical ranchero
and trader of the time—the weather, the crops, the livestock, the
government, the general economy.

He was a witness, along with his daughter Anita, at his son
John's marriage in Monterey on May 28, 1871, to 18-year-old
Martha Brawley, who had come out from Illinois with her parents and her twin sister Mary. John had taken over the responsibility for most of his father's affairs, as the latter was nearly 80
years old, an age considered far advanced, at that point in history.

A United States citizen once more by virtue of the treaty of
Guadalupe Hidalgo in 1848, Juan B.R. Cooper died at his San
Francisco home, February 9, 1872, and was buried from St.
Mary's Cathedral, Sunday, February 11.

His widow, Encarnacion, outlived him by nearly 30 years,
dying in San Francisco, January 15, 1902. She had also outlived
their son John, who died June 21, 1899, at Rancho El Sur. Still the
shadowy figure in the annals of the Cooper family, Encarnacion
had lived a very quiet life in San Francisco, helping her sister
Rosalia after the latter's husband, Jacob P. Leese, had died, and
spending most of her spare time with a small circle of Spanish-
speaking friends. Almost the only written records still extant,
disclosing her activities, consist of small charge accounts which
she ran up at the Nathan Spear store for trimming on clothes,
when her husband was away. Spear had also moved to and died in
San Francisco.

Two deeds transferring parts of the Sur ranch land to her
children and dated February 28, 1901, are signed by Encarnacion's "mark." On one of them her granddaughter, Frances Molera, states that she signed for her. Both deeds specify that Encarnacion was "unable to write."

Martha Brawley, the wife of John B. Henry Cooper, was born in Illinois, the daughter of John and Lucretia Brawley, and came with them to California. They lived for a time in Volcano, California, and then settled in the Castroville area, in time for the 1870 census. She married J.B. Henry Cooper May 28, 1871, at the age of 18. Witnesses signing the marriage certificate included Captain J.B.R. Cooper, Anita Cooper, David Spence, and a Cooper cousin, Celedonia Amesti. Martha lived into the 1940s, having remarried after her first husband's death. (Photo courtesy of Martha Cooper Lang.)

Maria Geronima Encarnacion Vallejo de Cooper. A photo taken during her later years. (Society of California Pioneers.)

California women of her generation and era for the most part did not have the advantages of schooling. When she needed to communicate with out-of-town friends she did so through some third party who could read and write, as is evidenced by a letter written to her from San Diego by Sarah J. King, wife of an Army surgeon who was stationed for two years in Monterey. Mrs. King acknowledged "your communication by Mr. Hamilton [another Army officer]" and expressed the hope that Encarnacion would return "a long answer" to her questions about recent events in Monterey.

A letter to Encarnacion from George Austin, written March 10, 1872, indicates that once again she had used an intermediary to correspond with him:

> Your letter of the 8th came to hand today requesting me to look well after the house which I do. I let nobody in the house except myself and Prisca [his wife]. She helps me sometimes to clean the house. The house is kept clean and nice just the same as when you left last. I open the windows upstairs in good weather every day and also the blinds down in front of the house and at any time you wish to come the house is clean and ready and I shall look out for everything the same as if it was my own and will let you know if anything happens.
>
> I am very sorry that Captain Cooper is dead. I have lost the best friend I ever had in the world and I feel it very much.

Nearly three years after Cooper's death, his fourth child and second daughter, Francisca Guadalupe Amelia, married Eusebio Joseph Molera, a graduate of the Royal Academy of Engineering in Madrid, who had left Spain for California in 1872 with a fellow student, J.C. Cebrian. After employment with the U.S. Lighthouse Engineers, Molera formed a partnership with Cebrian as civil engineers and architects, headquartered in San Francisco. He and his wife also divided responsibility for Rancho El Sur with John B.H. Cooper, who became a close friend of Molera.

The Moleras had two children: Andrew, born August 17, 1875, and Francesca, born Oct. 20, 1879. Neither of them married or had children.

Eusebio, who died January 14, 1932, in San Francisco, where he had served on the Board of Supervisors, outlived his son Andrew, who died October 8, 1931. His daughter, Francesca (Frances) died October 1, 1968.

After Anita Cooper Wohler had bought back the David Spence interest in the Cooper adobe in Monterey—Spence had deeded it to his wife, so that her sister, Mrs. Manuel (Luisa) Diaz, could continue to remain there during her lifetime—Anita willed it to her niece, Frances Molera, who had a doorway cut to add the one-story section to the two-story part, and installed a housekeeper who for many years cared for the house for Miss Molera. One room contained a large desk for the ranch records kept by Miss Molera's brother, Andrew. Eusebio Molera remodeled the building for his son's and daughter's use.

Miss Molera eventually willed the property to the National Trust for Historic Preservation, which in turn leased it to the California Department of Parks and Recreation, for complete restoration.

The State Parks Department bought at a reduced price from Frances Molera some 4,500 acres of the Rancho El Sur, to be named for her brother Andrew. Some 2,200 acres on the west side of Highway 1 were held by the Nature Conservancy until such a time as the Parks Department could acquire them. About 2,300 acres on the east side of the highway were acquired later.

All of the living descendants of Juan Bautista Rogers Cooper came through his first son, John Bautista Henry Cooper, and the latter's wife, Martha Brawley. They had four children.

(1) Alicia, born May 18, 1872, married twice, to Thomas Dillon, then to Frank Orcutt. She left one son, Jack Cooper Orcutt, who in turn left a daughter, Alicia Goodwin, who was living as of this writing in Orinda, Calif.

(2) John B.R. Cooper, named for his grandfather, born 1873, died 1948 in Carmel Valley. Married twice:

(a) to Mabel Ellsworth Green, November 8, 1900. They had two children: Isabel, born 1901, married and left two children, Hugh Ellsworth Knight and Isabel Frances Knight; second child Gladis, who left no children. She died February 23, 1962, in Carmel Valley, as wife of District Attorney Ed R. Barnes.

(b) Second marriage of John B.R. Cooper, (who was divorced from first wife) to Juanita Johnson. They had two children: Terezina Alicia, who married B. Aubrey Hackney. Mrs. Hackney and three adult sons, Alfred, John and Robert, are living in Marina; second child Martha, Mrs. Frank Lang, now widowed and living in Carmel Valley. She has an unmarried son,

Captain Cooper School, Big Sur, built on land donated by his granddaughter, Frances Molera.

John, and two daughters: Susie, now Mrs. John Richard Powers, living with husband and three sons in Carmel Valley; and Anne Marie Lang, now Mrs. Mark Rosen, also living in Carmel Valley.

(3) Abelardo Enos Cooper, third child of John B. Henry Cooper and Martha Brawley, was married to Elena Margarita Roach. They had two children:

(a) Viola, who died as a young woman, unmarried.

(b) Abelardo Henry Guadalupe, known as Juanie, living in Carmel Valley. He has a son, Robert, who has several children.

(4) Alfred H., died August 30, 1913, unmarried, at age 33, following an auto accident in Sur area.

The Historical and Biographical Record of Monterey and San Benito Counties noted that John B.R. Cooper, of Salinas, "has represented the district with honor as a member of the state legislature." He served with the 36th State Assembly. His father, John B.H. Cooper, had been chairman of the Monterey County Board of Supervisors and a member of that board for nine years.

The History of the State of California, by J.M. Guinn, 1910,
noted that John B.H. Cooper, in that position:

... safeguarded the interests of the taxpayer, while at the same time he favored
progressive measures for upbuilding the county ... Although death has termi-
nated his activities, it has not dimmed in the hearts of friends the memory of the
manly qualities possessed by Mr. Cooper ... At one time his landed possessions
aggregated 17,000 acres, which made him one of the largest land-owners in the
entire state. Included in his estate was the Moro Cojo Ranch, between Castroville and Salinas, a valuable property containing 12 large wells of fine water that
furnished complete irrigation facilities. After the Spreckels factory was established a portion of the ranch was devoted to beet culture and excellent returns
were realized from this crop. Another large estate owned by Mr. Cooper was the
San Bernabe Ranch of 13,000 acres near King City, the cultivation and management of which he personally superintended up to the time of his death ...

As soon as he was old enough to assume responsibilities his father had placed
him in charge of his ranch (El Sur) of 8,884 acres, where grain and stock were
raised and the dairy industry was conducted upon an extensive scale.

Of Captain Juan Bautista Rogers Cooper himself, the same
History of the State of California remarked that:

In his death the State lost one of its earliest American settlers, a man of
decided talent, rare executive ability and unsurpassed knowledge of seacraft ... It
has been said that the history of a state is the biography of the eminent men
thereof. Could there be written a full account of the life of Captain Juan Bautista
Rogers Cooper it would throw light upon the early days of California history ere
yet the state had become a portion of our commonwealth ...

The land was held in vast estates by Spaniards, who extended to him a
hospitality and friendship that won his esteem from the first. Through all his
life he remained a devoted champion of the old Spanish grandees, whose
passing marked the ascendancy of American interests along the coast ...

Gradually he began to acquire ranch lands and eventually he gave up the sea
for the more tranquil existence of a landsman, finding his chief pleasure in the
society of his family and in the care of his vast estates ...

The *Sacramento Daily Record* of February 14, 1872, quoting
the *San Francisco Bulletin* of two days earlier, said, "He was a
good man, always ready and willing to assist the unfortunate,
and, while quiet and unobtrusive, was kind and true to those with
whom he came in contact."

His brother-in-law, Mariano Vallejo, commenting in 1875,
three years after Cooper's death, said that "Encarnacion ... grate-

fully preserves the memory of that daring seaman, loyal friend
and excellent husband at whose side she passed 45 years without
a single disagreement."

And Governor Juan Bautista Alvarado, Cooper's nephew,
summed it all up in his statement that "in all and through all, he
contributed to the ennobling of his adopted country."

BIBLIOGRAPHY

The Blond Ranchero—Memories of Juan Francisco Dana. Dawson's Book Shop. Los Angeles, 1960.

Cleland, Robert Glass. *From Wilderness to Empire.* A history of California, 1542-1900. Knopf, New York, 1944.

Crossman, Carl. L. *The China Trade.* Foreword by Ernest S. Dodge. Pyne Press, Princeton, 1972.

Davis, William Heath. *Seventy Five Years in California.* John Howell, San Francisco, 1967.

de la Guerra, Angustias. *Occurrences in Hispanic California.* Translated and edited by Francis Price and William Ellison, Academy of American Franciscan History, Washington, D.C., 1956.

Dodge, Ernest S. *Beyond the Capes—Pacific Exploration from Captain Cook to the Challenger (1776-1877).* Little, Brown, Boston, Toronto, 1971.

Gast, Ross H. *Contentious Consul.* A biography of John Coffin Jones, first U.S. consular agent at Hawaii. Dawson's Book Shop, Los Angeles, 1976.

Gast, Ross H. *Don Francisco de Paula Marin.* A biography. Letters and journal edited by Agnes C. Conrad. University Press of Hawaii, Honolulu, 1973.

Gleason, Duncan and Dorothy. *Beloved Sister.* Arthur H. Clark Co., Glendale, CA, 1978.

Hawgood, John A., ed. *First and Last Consul: Thomas Oliver Larkin and the Americanization of California.* A selection of letters. Huntington Library Publications, San Marino, CA., 1962.

Holmes, Kenneth L. *Ewing Young: Master Trapper.* Binfords and Mort, Portland, OR., 1967.

Hunnewell, James. Honolulu in 1817 and 1818. *Papers of the Hawaiian Historical Society, #8.* Read before the Hawaiian Historical Society, July 18, 1895, by his son, James F. Hunnewell.

The Larkin Papers, for the History of California. University of California Press, Berkeley and Los Angeles, 1951-1968.

Loomis, Albertine. *Grapes of Canaan. Hawaii 1820.* Hawaiian Mission Children's Society, Honolulu, 1951.

Morgan, Dale L. *Jedediah Smith and the Opening of the West.* University of Nebraska Press, Lincoln, 1953.

Morrison, Samuel Eliot. *Maritime History of Massachusetts, 1783-1860.* Riverside Press, Cambridge, MA, 1921.

Nunis, Doyce B., Jr., ed. *The California Diary of Faxon Dean Atherton.* California Historical Society, San Francisco and Los Angeles, 1964.

Ogden, Adele. *The California Sea Otter Trade, 1784-1848.* University of California Press, Berkeley and Los Angeles, 1941.

Reynolds, Stephen. *The Voyage of the New Hazard to the Northwest Coast, Hawaii and China, 1810-1813.* Ye Galleon Press, Fairfield, WA. 1970.

148

The Roach-Belcher Feud. *California Historical Society Quarterly*, Vol. 29, San Francisco, 1950.

Robinson, W.W. *Land in California*. University of California Press, Berkeley and Los Angeles, 1979.

Rolle, Andrew F. *An American in California*. Henry E. Huntington Library, San Marino, CA. 1956.

Rolle, Andrew F. *California, a History*. Thomas Y. Crowell, New York. 1963

Simpson, Sir George. *Voyages to California Ports, 1841-42*. The Private Press of Thomas C. Russell, San Francisco, 1930

Sully, Langdon. *No Tears for the General. The Life of Alfred Sully, 1821-1879*. American West Publishing Co., Palo Alto, CA. 1974

Thomes, William H. *On Land and Sea*. DeWolfe, Fiske & Co., Boston, MA 1884.

Wright, Doris Marion. *A Guide to the Mariano Guadalupe Vallejo Documentos para la Historia de California 1780-1875*. Bancroft Library, University of California, Berkeley, 1953.

Wright, Doris Marion. *A Yankee in Mexican California: Abel Stearns, 1798-1848*. Wallace Heberd, Santa Barbara, 1977.

Library Sources

Baker Library, Harvard University, Cambridge, MA.
Bancroft Library, University of California, Berekeley, CA.
California Historical Society, San Francisco, CA.
California State Library, Sacramento, CA.
County of Monterey—Recorder's Office—Probates—etc., Salinas, CA.
Henry E. Huntington Library, San Marino, CA.
National Archives, Washington, D.C.
Peabody Museum, Salem, MA.
Hawaiian Mission Children's Society, Honolulu, Hawaii
Society of California Pioneers, San Francisco, CA.

A detailed list of sources would be as long as the book's text. The Larkin Papers and the Vallejo Documents have proven to be the main sources. This book on Cooper's life history is based largely on the records saved by his younger half-brother, Larkin, and his brother-in-law, Mariano Vallejo.

Index

150

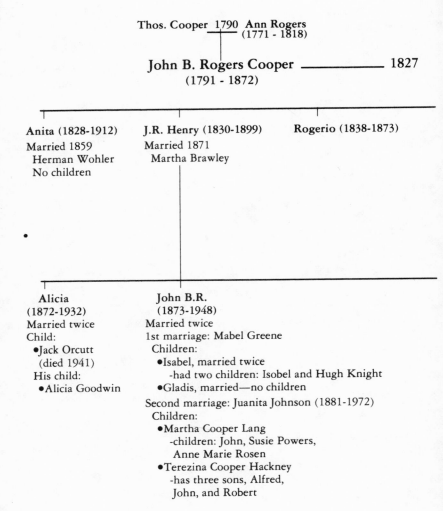

Thos. Cooper 1790 Ann Rogers
(1771 - 1818)

John B. Rogers Cooper ———————— 1827
(1791 - 1872)

Anita (1828-1912)
Married 1859
Herman Wohler
No children

J.R. Henry (1830-1899)
Married 1871
Martha Brawley

Rogerio (1838-1873)

Alicia
(1872-1932)
Married twice
Child:
 ●Jack Orcutt
  (died 1941)
 His child:
 ●Alicia Goodwin

John B.R.
(1873-1948)
Married twice
1st marriage: Mabel Greene
 Children:
 ●Isabel, married twice
  -had two children: Isobel and Hugh Knight
 ●Gladis, married—no children
Second marriage: Juanita Johnson (1881-1972)
 Children:
 ●Martha Cooper Lang
  -children: John, Susie Powers,
   Anne Marie Rosen
 ●Terezina Cooper Hackney
  -has three sons, Alfred,
   John, and Robert

For this chart only direct descendants of Captain Cooper and his wife Encarnacion have been listed. Both came from large families and collateral descendants are numerous.

The reader, however, should remember the close family ties of two men. Thomas O. Larkin, half brother of Cooper, came to Monterey to be his clerk, and